Contents

Foreword

The Promise of Information Marketing

by Dan Kennedy
NoBSBooks.com, DanKennedy.com

You Can Come to Interpret Marketing of Information With One of Two Mindsets

Here it is, plain and simple: This book tells you what you need to know and provides you with a practical, doable, realistic plan to harness all the powers of the internet, to sell information products, and to either begin or grow your information-marketing business to whatever size you want.

Who am I to make such a promise? Well, odd as it might seem at first, I'm not a fan of the internet, personally. In fact, I don't use it at all. I've never received or sent an e-mail and intend to go to my grave decades from now without doing so. I don't "surf the net" or visit websites. If I want to buy books from **Amazon.com**, I scribble their titles down on a piece of paper with a lead pencil and hand it to somebody. If I need to see a website, it's printed out for me on paper. In many ways, I think our society might be better off had this ever-expanding, ever-more-intrusive, ever-more-consuming thing Pandora kept locked in her box.

However, I have personally earned over $1 million a year for a number of years directly from e-commerce. Companies that I have interest in or that market my information products make extensive and sophisticated use of multiple websites and multiple types of websites, e-mail, blogs, community sites, webinars and affiliate marketing. For them and for my clients, I write sales copy for use online—and clients routinely pay me upward of $100,000 per project to do so. Combined, my businesses, the publishers of my products and my clients did well over $100 million in online sales in the most recent year. And, incidentally, many of the most celebrated and respected "gurus" of internet marketing are my followers, my private clients or members of my Platinum coaching group. My situation is direct demonstration of an important, basic, yet little-understood fact presented in this book: The internet is an advertising and marketing medium for information as well as an information delivery system. It doesn't require technical expertise or geeky love for it in order to use it as such a medium, any more than successfully selling things by direct mail requires knowing how to run printing presses or paper mills.

I am legendary as a truth-teller as a business advisor. In fact, the brand of my seven popular books and three newsletters is "NO BS." And I can caution you, the world of internet marketing is sadly awash in BS. That's why this book was so necessary and is so significant. It does *not* over-promise. It is *not* filled with untested ideas, idle boasting or weird and aberrant examples unreplicatable by average mortals. It is *not* an exercise in hype. Therefore, it does *not* promise you a four-minute workweek or money pouring out of your computer's printer on command. If you're looking for such fool's gold, you'll be disappointed. This is a book, a guide for serious businesspeople who take business seriously. It's filled—heck, overfilled—with actual, real-life, real-business examples from a diverse array of information businesses proving its principles and demonstrating its strategies. Its organizer, Robert Skrob, is the leader of *the* international trade association of the information marketing industry, a clearinghouse of "what's really working" second to none. Its co-author, Bob Regenerus, is an expert to whom I refer my own clients and has some businesses in which I own interests that I rely on. These guys are the real deal, and they have put together the real inside scoop.

For example, in this book they explain that the Holy Grail for websites is *not* more traffic, in contrast to most internet hype-sters who are constantly promoting the next traffic-building gimmick. Bragging rights to numbers of visitors are empty. In this book, they tell you how to target and attract the right kind of traffic, and how to convert it to customers and, more important, ongoing customer relationships. That's the real scoop. For example, they dare to discredit the most frequently seen, most popular and prevalent website designs and "looks," and reveal the one and only design strategy that really makes money. There is one thing you must do—that 99 percent of all web designers hate—and they reveal it. That's the real scoop. They even lay out real work you must do to make online information marketing work in this cluttered and competitive arena. It's work anyone can do. Still, it's courageous to show work to be done in this time when promises of riches for nothing are so popular. That's the real scoop.

I've spent 30 years in the information marketing business. I began and had my first big successes before there was the internet—or, for that matter, broadcast faxing or even capabilities comparable to the internet. The internet has minimized barriers of entry and startup, facilitated dirt-cheap market testing, removed all geographic boundaries, and crashed all speed limits. There has always been a little-noticed, little-understood, remarkably large population of independent info-marketers making millions from their kitchen tables and spare bedrooms, but the internet has contributed to the explosive growth of this population as well as enabled people to go from nice incomes to real wealth easier and faster than ever before.

Still, the internet is no panacea. Treating it as a business in and of itself rather than as a medium for building businesses is short-sighted. Being overly dependent on it is dangerous. I'm a firm advocate of online–offline integration. Like a handgun, in the right hands and used properly, it's useful and valuable. In the wrong hands, if it's used recklessly or ignorantly, somebody's gonna get hurt!

You can come to internet marketing of information from one of two mindsets. You can look for fast, cheap shortcuts and the making of a quick buck without regard to staying power and sustaining a business—sort of like riding into a frontier town, robbing its bank and riding out of town as fast as you can. Trouble is, few gunslingers lived to a ripe old age as wealthy men. Even Wyatt Earp died poor.

Or you can take a more measured, mature, intelligent approach. You can use tested and proven blueprints to develop solid, sustainable information publishing and marketing businesses with the internet as the driving force, both as a medium and as a delivery system. More like coming into a frontier town, doing the harder work of building homes and eventually shopping centers, and developing it from a single row of slapped-together bars and brothels on a muddy main street to a thriving metropolis. This book is the perfect guide for those interested in being business developers.

I hope you're of the latter mindset. If so, you'll find this book well worth its little price thousands of times over, and if perhaps you acquired it because of my name attached to it or my recommendation, you'll thank me for it.

Of course, this book is identical to its subject matter: the information marketing business and the internet itself—valueless without actions and implementation. So, I hope you don't merely read it and shelve it, but extract from it and act on it. That's why my colleagues and I write books. Not to use up trees, but to facilitate invention, innovation, action and development of thriving businesses. I hope yours is one of them. Happy e-commercing.

About the Authors

Robert Skrob started his first business when he was 23 years old. Today, at 36, he has become a serial entrepreneur in several industries. He personally publishes three newsletters a month for three different industries; one is 24 pages, another is 16 pages, and the last is a "quick read" newsletter at four pages. Robert is a lobbyist, advising his clients on strategies to get their ideas turned into laws. Plus, he plans several events, seminars and training programs involving multiple speakers each year. Robert's greatest skill is his marketing expertise. His first book, co-authored with Dan Kennedy and Bill Glazer, titled *The Official Get Rich Guide to Information Marketing: How to Build a Million Dollar Business Within 12 Months*, was published in November 2007 and topped the Barnes & Noble best-seller list as the number 2 business book. Robert conducts multiple internet marketing campaigns with more than 100 websites. Many of those sites have video, audio and electronic content delivery. Plus, Robert hosts a weekly national radio talk show, Business Profits Radio, teaching business owners how to make more money and spend less time in their businesses. Robert is married and has two kids. On weekends you can find him beside the pool or in the hot tub enjoying a mojito and a Partagas #10 cigar. You can find out more about Robert at his blog at **RobertSkrob.com**.

Bob Regnerus is a consultant, author, speaker, and entrepreneur, and one of the country's leading experts on internet marketing and website design. For over ten years, Bob has earned his reputation as "The Leads King" by helping his clients generate traffic for their websites and convert their website visitors into paying customers. His client list includes nationally-recognized brands, a wide variety of smaller businesses, and some of the world's most successful information marketers. Bob is always in demand as a public speaker, and he regularly travels the country to appear at seminars, events, and workshops. To learn more about Bob, visit **TheLeadsKing.com**.

About the Authors

Dan Kennedy is widely acknowledged as the leader in developing the modern information marketing industry. Certainly more people have gone from zero to multimillion-dollar info-businesses under his guidance than by any other means or mentor, and virtually every significant breakthrough in this industry in the last decade has come from Dan and his clients, including the now common continuity and forced continuity approaches, the ascension model, every means of selling high-priced coaching, boot camp add-on days, contests to promote coaching, and on and on and on. To learn how to use Dan's most recent breakthrough, info-marketers each paid $12,000 to attend a three-day briefing. Four different info-marketers pioneering this newest business model each went from zero to over $1 million in income within 12 months. Dan is the author of nine business books, including *No B.S. Direct Marketing for Non-Direct Marketing Businesses* and his newest, *No B.S. Time Management for Entrepreneurs*, available in bookstores or from online booksellers. Additional information and free chapter previews are available at **NoBSBooks.com**. Included with the book is a coupon for a free kit of peak personal productivity tools. Kennedy is also a busy entrepreneur, consultant, speaker, and direct-response advertising copywriter. Info is available at **DanKennedy.com.**

Chapter 1

Essentials of Information Marketing on the Internet

OR MOST AMERICANS THE INTERNET HAS REPLACED THE U.S. MAIL, the public library, the phone book, the road atlas, the cookbook, the dictionary, the encyclopedia and the textbook. When people want information, they go to the internet first. And of all the different things people can do on the internet, most of them are doing just one: looking for information. There's never been a better time to be in the internet information marketing business.

Internet information marketing is responsive to and fueled by the ever-increasing pressure on people's time. Businesspeople and consumers alike need information provided to them in convenient forms, and in some cases, need an extension of it. Methods and strategies for information searches that might merely have been taught to them 10 years ago are now done for them by the internet.

The information industry encompasses products such as traditional books, audio programs, videos or DVDs that you might buy in a store, from a catalog or online; magazines; newsletters; e-books;

membership websites; tele-seminars and webinars; tele-coaching programs; and seminars and conferences—and combinations thereof.

The possible topics are almost endless. People buy information on every imaginable subject, from better sex, to teaching parrots to talk, to gardening, to investing in real estate foreclosures, to running businesses.

Information marketing, then, is about identifying a responsive market with high interest in a particular group of topics and expertise, packaging information products and services matching that interest (written/assembled by you or by others, or both), and devising ways to sell and deliver it. If you can name it, somebody is packaging and profitably selling information about it.

The development of the internet has been good for every type of business. It lets companies advertise in new ways, sell more products to more people, keep better track of their inventory and provide better customer service. It has even created a market for companies that couldn't exist otherwise, some of which, like Google, eBay and Amazon, bring in billions of dollars a year. Of all the opportunities the internet provides, though, the most exciting are the opportunities for information marketers because they're the people who sell what everyone else is looking for.

If you have an information marketing business now, you can't afford to miss out on what the internet has to offer. If you're just getting started in information marketing, the internet will help you make your first sale more quickly and with less risk.

Six Reasons the Internet Is Perfect for Information Marketing

Let's take a look at six specific reasons the internet is such a great medium for information marketers.

Reason #1: You Can Get Started for Nothing

One of the best things about internet information marketing is the ease with which you can start doing it.

If you already have an information marketing business, the internet allows you to expand into a giant new market without diverting resources or hiring a dozen new employees. If you're not in business already but you have an information product to sell, you can get started without going thousands of dollars into debt.

Think about all the things you have to buy or rent before you start a traditional company. Depending on your business model, you'll need an office, a storefront or a reliable car. You'll need to buy mailing lists, and you'll need to spend money on advertising and promotion. You might also have to pay franchise fees or hire employees. Before you've even had a chance to make your first sale, you could be out tens of thousands of dollars.

On the other hand, if you use the internet, you can start selling right away. There's no need to rent office space, build a home office— or even buy a computer. If you don't have internet access at home, you can go to the public library and get online for free.

In fact, you don't even have to wait until you have an e-book, a newsletter or other finished product. All you have to do is sign up for a free blog and start writing. If you know your subject matter and you know what your audience wants to see, you'll attract attention and establish yourself as an expert. Once you've accomplished that, all you have to do is decide how to build your business and cash in. There are plenty of ways to do that, and when you've finished this book, you'll know what the options are and how to take advantage of each one.

Reason #2: The Market Has No Boundaries

Traditional businesses are limited by their distance from their customers, but there's no such thing as distance on the internet. No matter where in the world a person lives, if he or she has access to a computer and an internet connection, your website is only a few keystrokes away. You can advertise to customers in Japan as easily as you can advertise to the people who live around the corner.

Does marketing on the internet mean that you can expect to sell your product to everyone on earth? Of course not. But it does mean you'll reach more people than you could through any other medium, and as you're about to see, it means you'll be able to sell products that wouldn't otherwise be marketable.

Reason #3: It's Cost-Effective to Market Low-Demand Items

A few years ago, statisticians announced that the world's population had grown to over 6 billion, and TV talk show hosts all made the same joke. Even if you have a one-in-a-million personality, they said, there are 6,000 other people exactly like you.

Well, more than 1 billion people use the internet, and that number grows every day. So, even if only one person in a thousand will be interested in your product, you have more than a million potential customers out there.

If you didn't have a website, one-in-a-thousand demand wouldn't do you much good. You could never make a profit if you had to knock on a thousand doors to make one sale, or if a thousand people walked through your store for every one who took something off the shelf.

When you use the internet, it becomes possible to make money with low-demand products through the magic of niche marketing.

In 2006, Chris Anderson published a fantastic book about niche marketing called *The Long Tail*. In the book he explains that because internet merchants have lower storage and distribution costs, they're able to sell low-demand products at a profit.

If you want a quick demonstration, compare the number of titles available on Netflix, Amazon or iTunes with the number of titles available in your local video store, bookstore or record store. The local stores can only afford to stock items that are likely to be very popular because the stores have a limited amount of shelf space. A title that might sell once a month would take up room that could be occupied by something that sells several times a day.

Netflix, Amazon and iTunes, on the other hand, don't have to pay for storefront space. Their websites serve as their stores, and the merchants only spend money on shipping and a few centralized warehouses (iTunes doesn't even have those expenses). When millions of customers are shopping in one "store," it becomes possible to make money on items that appeal to only 1 customer in 100 or 1 in 1,000.

"Low demand" is much different from "no demand." You'll find that there's a lot of money to be made using the internet to sell products that no one else offers.

Reason #4: Delivery Is Effortless

The internet has lowered distribution costs for book merchants and video rental services, but it has practically eliminated those costs for information marketers. Two online delivery methods, the e-book and the membership site, make it easy for even the smallest marketing business to distribute products to customers all over the world.

E-Books. There's always going to be a place for paper books in the information marketing world and in the world of publishing as a whole. In fact, a recent publishing industry survey predicted that paper book sales will continue to increase over the next few years.

However, the electronic book, or e-book for short, is changing the way people read and the way people publish. The e-book is a fantastic tool for people who are just getting started in information marketing or who want to add a new twist to their product lines.

The most obvious benefit of the e-book is the publishing cost: there is none. Assuming that you already have word processing software on your computer, all you have to do is sit down, write and hit the "Save" button.

You can distribute your e-book in any format, but your best bet is to convert it into a PDF file, which ensures that it will display correctly no matter what type of computer your reader is using. If you don't have the software to create PDF files, you can buy Adobe Acrobat for a few hundred bucks, or you can find a free program to do the same job.

Once you have your e-book finished, you can sell (or give away) thousands of copies, and you won't pay anything for distribution (unless you count the cost of your website hosting). That definitely beats spending thousands of dollars to self-publish a traditional book.

E-books aren't only for people who lack the cash to publish a paper book. In February 2008, Suze Orman, one of the world's most famous and successful information marketers, appeared on the Oprah Winfrey Show. She announced that her book *Women and Money* would be available online as a free e-book for 33 hours. More than 1 million people downloaded the book in those 33 hours.

Now, why would Suze Orman want to do that, given that her book was already selling well in bookstores? It's pretty simple, really. Before you could actually start the download, you had to submit your name and address to the website Suze was using to distribute the e-book. That means that Suze now has more than *1 million extra names* on her customer list, and she can use that list to promote everything she writes in the future. There's no way her publisher would have let her give away a million hardcover books, but since e-books don't cost anything, there was no downside. Suze and her publisher probably lost out on a few hardcopy sales of *Women and Money*, but they'll more than make up for it by selling to that huge e-mail list.

Another thing that makes e-books so appealing is their flexibility. Traditional publishers can't afford to publish very short or very long books, and customers tend to shy away from anything outside the traditional range. There are no restrictions on the size of an e-book, however. We've bought e-books that were as short as seven or eight pages, and we've bought some that were as long as 700 or 800 pages.

E-books let you tailor your product to the needs of the material, without worrying about economics or outdated expectations.

Membership Sites. Membership websites are the next step in the evolution of online information marketing. With a membership site, you're not only making a one-time sale to a customer; you're getting them to pay once a year or even once a month for access to your website.

Membership sites aren't new, but they're becoming more popular with information marketers for a couple of reasons. In the past, the software necessary to maintain a membership site was expensive, restrictive and difficult to use. In the past few years, several less expensive products have become available, and these products automate most of the processes that used to require an administrator's intervention.

More important, internet users are drawn to online communities. People love to interact on social networking sites like MySpace and Facebook, in discussion forums and in the comment areas of blogs. A good membership website provides users the same ability to interact. Information marketers can't afford to pass up the opportunity to create a specialized community for their customers.

When you have a membership site, your ability to connect with your customers is almost unlimited. You can keep track of how often individuals visit your site, and you'll be able to see what types of content they gravitate toward, which will help you make better offers to them.

The Automatic Cash Register. Automated order-taking and fulfillment are two other huge benefits of doing business online. When you're running a traditional business, you or your employees have to be involved in every transaction. You have to take your customer's order, collect payment and get the product in the mail.

When you use a website to sell your product, your customers enter all the necessary information themselves and your website handles the delivery. Whether you're selling memberships, e-books or other online products, you can make sales anywhere, at any time, without lifting a finger.

Reason #5: You Get Immediate Feedback

Information marketers like to test things. We like to test products and services to find out which are most appealing to our customers. We like to test different price levels and price structures to get a sense of what the market will support. We like to test copy in our marketing materials to find the best way to connect with the public.

The internet allows you to collect feedback immediately, as opposed to the days or weeks required for offline campaigns. This means you can test more things more often, and you'll get more reliable results.

Let's say you're planning a new direct marketing campaign and, as a first step, you're going to send a sales letter to 5,000 homes. You've come up with two potential headlines for the sales letter, but you're not sure which one will be more effective. To find out, you print two versions of the letter. You'll send 2,500 letters with one headline, send 2,500 with the other headline and wait to find out which generates more responses.

There are three main difficulties with that sort of test. First, you're looking at a full week, probably two weeks, before you can expect any measurable response. When you do start getting responses, keeping track of which letter went to which customer is going to be a difficult and labor-intensive process. Also, you can't actually know how many people opened the letter, so you can't have any certainty that your nonresponses are traceable to the headline.

On the other hand, if you send that letter via e-mail, it will be delivered immediately, and you'll start getting responses within minutes. It's the easiest thing in the world to include a slightly different link in the two versions of the e-mail so when people respond to it (meaning they click on the link you've included), you'll always know which version they received. E-mail doesn't solve the third problem—knowing whether people actually read the letter—but there are other online tools that let you compare the number of people who see an offer compared with the number who respond.

We're not trying to convince you that offline marketing is a thing of the past. You may very well need to supplement your online marketing with direct mail, print, radio and television advertising. The point is, the internet has a place in those efforts as well. The testing you do online will help you improve every aspect of your marketing campaign.

Naming The 4-Hour Workweek. Tim Ferriss has a great story that illustrates this point. Tim has become a worldwide sensation thanks to his bestselling book *The 4-Hour Workweek*, and he owes that success, at least in part, to internet marketing feedback.

The original title of Tim's book was *Selling Drugs for Fun and Profit*. The book was finished, and Tim's publisher was ready to go to print, but Tim decided to do a little extra research first. Tim ran an internet marketing campaign using one of his alternate titles, *The 4-Hour Workweek*, and he found that his audience responded favorably to that title. In fact, when he compared those results to the results he achieved with any other title, including *Selling Drugs for Fun and Profit*, he realized that *The 4-Hour Workweek* was the runaway winner.

It took a little pushing before he convinced his publisher to change the title, but he got it done, and the book went straight to the top of *The New York Times* bestseller list. Obviously, the book has a lot of things going for it in addition to a good title, but Tim put himself at a great advantage by using a title he already knew would grab the attention of his audience.

You can use that same strategy in your own business. Using the internet, you can track the effectiveness of almost every step in the marketing process. You can (and should) experiment with your ad copy on Google AdWords, the text on your website, your prices, your offers and your products. What you learn in those experiments will help you create more effective offline advertising and help you refine your sales process.

Reason #6: Additional Revenue Sources

Another major benefit to information marketing on the internet is the possibility of generating additional revenue by participating in affiliate programs or selling advertising space. These programs aren't right for everyone, and they can actually work against you if you let them interfere with your core business. Under the right circumstances, though, they can give a nice boost to your bottom line.

Affiliate Programs. Affiliate programs let you refer customers to other websites and collect commissions on the purchases they make. Amazon pioneered this concept in the 1990s, and since then it has become a fundamental part of electronic commerce.

When you act as an affiliate, you place a text link or banner ad on your website that leads to the website of the merchant you're affiliated with. When your website visitors click on the link or ad, they're taken to the merchant's website, and if they buy something, you get a commission. Commissions from the big names like Amazon are usually below 10 percent, but you may be able to get a larger percentage if you work with a smaller merchant.

You can get started in affiliate marketing by signing up with one specific merchant, or you can join an affiliate network, which works as a broker to bring website owners and merchants together. Either way, it only takes a few minutes to set up the arrangement, and you can start earning extra money right away.

Affiliate marketing is a two-way street, by the way. Starting your own affiliate program and paying other website owners to refer their visitors to you is a great way to increase your web traffic and find good sales leads. We discuss that strategy in detail in Chapter 8.

AdSense Advertising. You can make extra money by selling ad space on your website. The idea here is similar to affiliate marketing, but you're not collecting a commission based on sales. To sell advertising space, you simply sign up with an ad-serving program like Google AdSense. The ad server chooses the ads that appear on your site, and you collect a fee based on the number of people who view or click on the ad.

Google AdSense is certainly not the only ad server out there, but it's the biggest one, and as with many tools on the internet, it's best to start with Google. AdSense ads are plain text, so they're less distracting than the banner ads you might get from other programs.

Again, this isn't for everyone. Advertising for other websites can distract your visitors or take them away from your site before you've had a chance to sell to them. There's a time and a place to sell ad space, and there's a time to sell your own products and services. Don't try to do both at once.

> For a complete worksheet to help you organize your internet information marketing business, walk you through the process step-by-step and help you make money more quickly, visit **InternetInfoMarketing Book.com/start-up.**

What This Book Is Not

We want you to come in with the right expectations, so let's talk for a minute about what this book is *not*.

This book is not an introduction to information marketing. We assume that you're already in the industry or, at minimum, know what information marketing is. If you need to start with the basics, pick up *The Official Get Rich Guide to Information Marketing*, which provides a comprehensive overview of the industry.

Nor is this book a guide to starting an information marketing business. We assume you've identified your target market and you have an information product to sell. If you need help researching a market or identifying an opportunity, read Chapter 2 of *The Official Get Rich Guide to Information Marketing*. If you need help figuring out what type of information product to create, read Chapter 3 of *The Official Get Rich Guide to Information Marketing*. For even more help on these questions, read *Entrepreneur Magazine's Start-Up Guide to Information Marketing*.

Our focus here is on using the internet to build and enhance your business. If you're ready to take advantage of the unique opportunities the internet provides to information marketers, this book tells you everything you need to know.

For a free evaluation of your internet marketing plan, visit **TheLeadsKing. com/quiz-page**.

$180,000 Worth of Inspiration

This is one of our favorite information marketing success stories. It illustrates two of the key points we've tried to make in this introduction: 1) online information marketing requires almost no start-up cost, and 2) you can make money even if you do the little things wrong.

Tracey and Dan are a married couple who live in Kentucky. Tracey ran a candle-making business from home, and she thought she might be able to supplement her business by writing a book. So in her spare time she typed up a 100-page book on how to make candles.

When Tracey finished the book, Dan converted it to PDF format and registered a website domain name. Next, he built a website to sell Tracey's book as an e-book, and he opened an account on Google AdWords to drive traffic to the website.

At that point, they were in business, and it only cost them $47 to get there. Here's the breakdown of that $47:

■ Writing the e-book: $25. Tracey had all the candle-making

knowledge she needed, so her only out-of-pocket expense was the price of a style guide to help her with her writing.

- Web domain registration: $7 for the first year at **GoDaddy.com.**
- Hosting for the website: $10 per month.
- AdWords account activation: $5 one-time fee.
- Website design: $0. Dan designed the site himself (it showed, but we'll get to that in a minute).
- PayPal account: $0. Like many information marketers, Dan and Tracey use a free PayPal account to accept payments for their products.

Now Dan isn't a web designer and he isn't a copywriter. The website he set up to sell Tracey's e-book was far from professional. It was not great to look at, it didn't have any special features and the text needed a lot of polish. It had a few things going for it, though. It got straight to the point and told visitors what Tracey's e-book had to offer, and it connected with visitors by demonstrating the passion Tracey had for the subject. As you'll learn, those are the things that really matter.

Things moved slowly at first, but Dan and Tracey didn't get discouraged. Dan kept working to improve his AdWords campaign and his website, and soon enough, the sales started trickling in. Within a few months, they had a full-fledged information marketing business on their hands. They were selling 10 books a week, and they had established themselves as a presence in the market. They took advantage of that foothold by selling additional products through affiliate sales programs. They were making over $1,500 a month, and 80 percent of that was profit. Their only ongoing costs were hosting for the website and pay-per-click fees from AdWords.

Now, think about what Dan and Tracey invested to earn that extra $1,500 a month in income. A little bit of time, $47 and 5 or 10 cents per click from AdWords. Compare that to the investment they'd have to make in the stock market to get the same return. Even if you assume an increase of 10 percent per year (and that's wishful thinking these days), you're talking about an initial investment of $180,000.

So which would you rather do? Wait until you have an extra few hundred thousand dollars to invest or use your knowledge to start earning money now? If the second option sounds better to you, keep reading. This book tells you step by step how to use the internet to capitalize on your experience and enthusiasm.

How Bob Regnerus Went From Techno Geek to "The Leads King"

Info-Marketer Profile

Before becoming "The Leads King" and co-author of this internet information marketing book, Bob Regnerus was a techno geek. "I was a programmer, and I started my career working on mainframe computers at a large corporation," Bob explains. "I transitioned from that over the years, and in the late 1990s, I started applying my programming skills to the internet, learning how to do e-commerce stores, similar to **Amazon.com**. I started developing websites and e-commerce sites for clients—I was the web guy."

The "web guy" soon turned into a "marketing guy."

"Clients started coming to me and saying, 'You know, I've got this great site and I'm selling products, but I don't know how to get traffic to my site.' The first thing I did was say, 'Yeah, I can do it for you.' Then I had to go figure out how to do it!" Bob laughs.

Bob started studying internet marketing. The first product he bought was from Corey Rudl. "Corey's information product was geared toward internet marketing," Bob recalls, "and I started studying the model of how to generate traffic, how to sell things online, and then I started applying those principles to my clients. I also wrote computer applications and learned how to sell them online and did fairly well."

➡

Bob became known for his affiliate software program that managed affiliate relationships and kept track of visitors: "I wrote a program for a client and maintained the license for it. I actually started marketing it as my own product and as a stand-alone application that people could purchase and install on their websites."

Soon it occurred to Bob that he could become an affiliate himself, so he began promoting other people's products and learning how to use Google AdWords. Eventually, he became an expert in generating traffic to websites and was able to profit on other people's products because he knew how to generate traffic better than the publishers could themselves. "Affiliate relationships are great strategies for a lot of companies because many publishers who aren't as well versed in generating traffic or who are interested in increasing distribution will use affiliates to bring additional traffic they couldn't get themselves," he says.

In 2004, Bob attended Bill Glazer and Dan Kennedy's "Information Marketing Summit." Bob recalls, "Bill threw out a comment, saying, 'Well, this product is really for people who are looking to make a million dollars a year and more.' I wasn't even near to making that kind of money, and I thought, 'Wow! Yeah, that's me.' I went back to my hotel room and actually wrote Bill a sales letter about my application and told him why he should take on this green internet marketing rookie who wanted to get deeper into this whole world. I have been part of Bill's mastermind group ever since."

A dare from the mastermind group led Bob into the successful business he enjoys today: "After hearing me talk about how I was generating traffic for websites as an affiliate, my mastermind members said, 'Bob, you don't need to be doing this for yourself. You need to be doing it for these other guys. You need to be doing it for me.' So, I started serving members from the coaching group and doing all their traffic for them."

Today, Bob's business has five employees and more than three dozen contractors serving his information marketing clients. "Information marketers need leads, and they understand that they need to feed their front-end funnels. We're able to do that for them, and we get the paid traffic and the free traffic. We have pay-per-click experts on staff, search engine optimization experts on staff and designers on staff to help them develop high-quality converting landing pages," Bob explains.

Bob's business is a one-stop shop for info-marketers who want to fill their front-end funnels using the internet, and now he's expanding it to other industries where lead generation is necessary. "Maybe it's not necessarily to get a free report," Bob explains, "but they are looking for the phone to ring, or they are looking to book an appointment. Any type of industry that's focusing on generating leads is where we're finding we have generated the most excitement among clients."

Bob's client roster includes prestigious institutions like the Dartmouth School of Business, Miracle-Ear®, dental professionals, chiropractors, information marketers, real estate investors, CPAs, chiropractors, restaurant owners, authors, consultants, coaches, speakers, cosmetic surgeons, martial arts schools, online retailers, construction companies, business colleges, e-book publishers, entertainers, e-tailers, clothing stores, supply companies, weight loss solutions, golf schools, voice talents, business opportunity seekers, financial experts and many more.

"The principles of lead generations don't change from market to market," Bob says. "You have to be out there with the right kind of message that matches what's going on in the prospect's head, giving them something of value to generate that lead."

Bob promotes his business primarily through referrals.

"Nothing is more valuable than having one of your clients excited enough to pick up the phone and contact their colleague and say, 'You need to work with Bob because of what he's doing.' Our best converting clients are still coming in through referrals. We also have quite a few joint ventures with information marketers that have a lot of clients in their herds, and we are developing services and programs for them."

Bob also promotes his services by providing written content to online and offline publications about lead generation techniques. "There are so many publications out there that are just starving for this type of content," Bob explains. "Writing this content and having it published is setting our company up as the obvious expert. It breaks down the barriers to bringing in new business because the client or the prospect is already convinced of your credibility and your authority. It just becomes a matter of them coming to you with money in hand and saying, 'Please do this for us.'"

The first thing Bob does with new clients is to make sure they understand that lead generation is not about "going straight from the first date to marriage."

"A lot of clients think they have only one shot at a prospect, and they basically ask for marriage right up front," Bob says. "We work with clients to help them understand there is a process from moving a website visitor to a prospect and then the prospect to a customer."

Using a two-step or multistep process, Bob teaches his clients to offer something of value to the website visitor. If the visitor takes the offer, that visitor becomes a prospect, and Bob tells his clients to follow up with that prospect for as long as he or she is willing to accept communication.

Getting visitors to accept that first offer is the key, and Bob ➡

teaches several strategies for making that happen. "For people just starting out, we want them to establish themselves in some way and to have an online presence," he explains. "Some people still don't have a website, or the website they have is inadequate. For example, if we are working with a dentist in Chicago, we'll set up a website called **ChicagoDentalPractice.com** and have them start a blog with content of interest to dentists in that area."

Bob has his clients write brief articles, posting them on their blogs and distributing them through article directories such as **EasyArticles.com**. Another marketing strategy Bob recommends is seeking out forums and other blogs where prospective clients are gathered and then making comments or entering questions. "There are a lot of forums out there," he says. "For example, in the dental community, there are forums where people are looking for an answer to a specific problem they're having. We are teaching our clients to go ahead and start answering some of those questions, making comments at people's blogs, and within your comments or within your post, you post a link back to your website."

According to Bob, participating in blogs and other online forums does two things: "Number one, it gets people to see that you have credibility and authority, and they'll actually click on the link if it's a forum or a blog that has a lot of traffic. The second thing is, the search engines will start to see those links and will actually increase your website's search engine ranking because more people are 'voting for your site' by seeing that link. So we are able to increase not only human visitor traffic, but also search engine traffic."

Another strategy Bob recommends to his more established clients is to use pay-per-click services. "We will always start with Google AdWords (**Google.com/adwords**)," Bob says. "This allows you to learn the keywords your prospects are typing in or looking for and the ones that are generating response. It's very important to track what you are doing. Going back to my dentist example, I might bid on the term *Chicago dentist*, but I also might type in and offer solutions to *tooth infection* or *jaw pain*. If you are tracking this properly, you'll start to see which words generate the most traffic to your website."

Learning which words generate the most website traffic can improve marketing by putting those messages out to the marketplace. Bob refers to this as having "market intelligence."

"Knowing key words can help you focus your message and create offers based on what people are searching for. Once you know what people really want, you can take that information and use it in all of your marketing, not just in your online promotions," Bob says.

Chapter 2

The Power of
ONE

CLARITY OF PURPOSE IS THE MOST IMPORTANT MARKETING PRINCIPLE. Before you begin any direct marketing campaign, it's critical to get a clear understanding of the purpose of each component. Too many marketers try to create an ad that both sells a product and does brand building. Their efforts are doomed to fail at both. When it comes to getting responses from your website visitors, ONE is the magic number. When you present your visitors with ONE yes-or-no decision at a time, you're more likely to get the results you want.

Why one decision at a time? Because when people arrive at your website, they're in a state of confusion, impatience and indecision. They've already done several internet searches and sifted through the results. They've already visited some of your competitors' sites, and they expect to look at several more before they find what they're looking for. They're not in the mood to read everything on your site. They just want to know, right away, whether you can help them.

The Power of ONE allows you to answer that question with a yes and keep your visitors on your site. When you use the Power of ONE, you simplify the experience for your website visitors and guide them toward the goal. No matter what you want from your visitors, you increase your chances of getting it when you ask simply and directly.

This strategy is one of the first things we teach our clients, and it's the first strategy we're going to discuss in this book. Why? Because it's something you have to understand before you even start designing (or fixing) your website. If you don't plan your website with the right goal in mind, you'll never use it to its full advantage.

Why You Need the Power of ONE

One thing all internet marketers want to avoid is a "bounce." A bounce happens when a visitor looks at a website and immediately closes the browser window or clicks back to the last page he or she was on. If you want to accomplish anything with your website, you have to avoid bounces and convince people to interact with your site. It's not as easy as it sounds—some websites lose over half their visitors to bounces. Just getting a response, a click on any link on your site, is a victory in itself.

Getting that first click is a hollow victory, though, if it's not on the right link. The ultimate goal of your website is to make a sale, so you want all activity on your site to lead to that goal. If you have lots of links and lots of distracting content on your site, you may convince people to click on a few links, but you probably won't get them any closer to making a purchase.

Websites that lead visitors through a series of simple yes-or-no decisions are the most effective websites for two reasons: they get *more* responses from visitors, and they get more of the *right kind* of responses.

In this chapter, we look at the problems you'll run into if you don't provide a simple experience for your visitors, and we go through the steps of planning a website that truly harnesses the Power of ONE.

Too Many Choices = Indecision

The more choices you put in front of people, the longer it will take them to make a decision and the less likely they are to be happy with the choice they make. When the number of options gets really overwhelming, people often respond by making no decision at all.

Cable and satellite TV illustrate this point well. When we were growing up, we had four channels to choose from: three networks and a public television station. Now, we're not saying that we'd like to give up ESPN, CNN or the other 300 channels we get today, but part of us misses the simplicity of TV in the old days.

Back then, we always knew what was on every station, and if we didn't like the shows, we just didn't watch TV. Nobody ever sat in front of the set for hours on end, flipping through those same four channels, grumbling that there was nothing on. Today, you can never be sure that what's on the screen is the best possible option, and if you don't know in advance what you want to watch, you're in for a long night of channel-hopping.

Internet users already face the same problem, multiplied by a factor of millions. There are more than 20 billion web pages on the internet right now, and the number grows daily. Looking for one specific answer in that sea of information can be time-consuming, confusing and frustrating. The last thing you want to do is force your visitors to do more work once they get to your site.

You have to assume that the people who come to your website have been searching for an answer for hours. Their fingers are tired, and their eyes are glazed over. They aren't paying close attention to everything on the screen. Your goal is to make things easy for them, and the best way to do that is to offer a simple yes-or-no decision.

Gone in Seven Seconds. One of the most important things we've learned in our years of research is that it only takes internet users three to seven seconds to decide whether they're interested in a website.

Think about that: three to seven seconds. It took longer than that to read the last paragraph. It's almost no time at all, but if you don't do something in those first few seconds to grab your visitors' attention, you're going to lose them.

You may have the perfect solution to your visitors' problem, but if you bury that solution behind menus, directories and unrelated links, it will take them more than seven seconds to find it. That means, more often than not, your visitors will be gone before they see what you have to offer.

Websites that use the Power of ONE grab their visitors' attention and snap them out of their trance. These websites announce clearly and boldly what they're about. They don't make their visitors sit through a 20-second intro before the real page opens. They don't play distracting animated sequences or background music. Most of all, effective websites don't present their visitors with a page full of choices. They present a single idea and let visitors decide whether it's the idea they're interested in.

Too Many Choices = Misunderstanding

Simplifying your website will do more than help your visitors make a decision. It will also assure your visitors that they're actually on the website they intended to visit. That may sound like a minor point, but it's not. Misunderstanding is just as effective as indecision when it comes to driving visitors away from a website.

If you fail to immediately establish your identity, your visitors will assume they clicked on the wrong link or they were taken in by a misleading advertisement or a phony website description. Those hazards are familiar to every internet user, and your visitors probably ran into a few of them before they got to your site, so they won't give you the benefit of the doubt.

Your web address is not enough to verify that your site is the site your visitors wanted to see. Plenty of websites use addresses that have nothing to do with the site content in an attempt to attract traffic they don't really deserve. These sites make money by collecting ad revenue, so their only goal is to get their pages to open in someone's browser. It makes no difference to them if the visitor clicks away immediately—they've made their money. If anything on your site gives your visitors a reason to think your site is one of those, they'll leave without a second thought.

The key here is to remember how your visitors are coming to your website. Most of them aren't there because they're already familiar with you or your business. They're on your site because they clicked on an advertisement, an internet search result or a link on someone's website. Something led them to believe you might have the answer they're looking for, and it's your job to confirm that belief.

Let's say, for example, that you're selling information related to diabetes control. Your visitors are people who did a search on Google or another search engine for something like "diabetes control" or "diabetes cure" or "diabetes information." Either your website appeared in the search results or your ad appeared on the search results page or a link appeared on one of the other sites your visitors checked out. Don't worry about the mechanics right now—we'll talk about how to make those things happen in Chapter 8.

The point is, whichever source brought your visitors in, they're expecting to see something related to diabetes control. More specifically, they're expecting to see the words *diabetes* and *control*. You have to make sure those words appear on the page, and you can't expect your visitors to search for them.

Every page on your website should include a large, compelling headline that welcomes the visitor and describes the message on the page. When you harness the Power of ONE, the first words your visitors see will assure them you have the information they want.

Too Many Choices = Aimless Visitors

There's one more reason to use the Power of ONE: keeping your visitors in the right areas of your website.

A website that offers too many choices gives visitors too many opportunities to get lost in unproductive pursuits. If you really want to turn your visitors into customers, you need to focus their attention on the ONE action that will get them closer to that goal.

To demonstrate the importance of focusing your visitors' attention, let's take a quick look at the world's two most popular search engines.

The Value of the Power of ONE on the Internet

Between the two of them, Google and Yahoo! account for 80 percent of the internet searches done in the United States. Both companies offer dozens of other products and services, but they make their money by selling ad space next to their search engine results. The more search requests they get, the more money they make.

Let's see how these two sites present their main sources of revenue—their search forms. We'll start with Yahoo!.

Yahoo! has always used the "web portal" model, meaning that it provides directories and lists in addition to search results (Figure 2-1, next page). On its front page, we see a list of about 20 content categories on the left side, a pair of news modules (four tabs apiece, with about a dozen links per tab) in the middle of the page and a few large ads and customizable sections along the right side.

It might take a minute to find the actual search form among all the images, ads and links, so we'll just point out that it's along the top margin of the screen, to the right of the company logo.

Now, let's look at how Google does it.

FIGURE 2-1. Because of Yahoo!'s "web portal" business model, there are dozens of links for a user to choose from.

It's a little easier to find the search form here, isn't it? It's right in the middle of the screen, where your eyes look first after the page opens. There are no ads, no images other than the Google logo and only a handful of other links (Figure 2-2, page 28).

Is it any wonder that Google surpassed Yahoo! as the dominant search engine after only a few years of existence? Is it a surprise that Google now gets three times as many search requests as Yahoo! or that Google's profits were six times higher than Yahoo!'s in 2007?

FIGURE 2-2. Google's front page illustrates that it understands the Power of ONE. Google.com understands that its user wants a clutter-free web search. Google.com provides that with a simple dialog box.

Google owes its success to two things: innovative technology and an understanding of what its users want. You hear plenty about Google's search formula, but its page design is just as important.

When people are looking for an answer to a question, they want to find it as quickly as possible—they don't want to read entertainment news, and they don't want to be distracted by video advertisements. If Google clutters up its search page with a bunch of extra content, we bet it will lose its number-one ranking.

This is not to say there's no place for information portals. Yahoo! may not be the most popular search engine, but it's still the most visited website overall, and it does turn a decent profit. You may have a reason to provide lots of information (or links to information) on your website, and we won't tell you not to.

What we will tell you is that you shouldn't provide all your information to people who are visiting your website for the first time. First-time visitors, the people who get to your site by clicking on an advertisement or search-engine result, have to be dealt with in a specific way. You, not they, need to control the process. If you lead your potential customers through a sequence of yes-or-no decisions, you'll increase your sales and keep your customers happier.

Harnessing the Power of ONE

Before you build a website that harnesses the Power of ONE, you need to set your goals and develop your plan. Don't rush through these steps. You may want to get your site up and running as soon as possible, but you need to think it through first to ensure that you wind up with the right type of website.

Your Sales Funnel

A marketing campaign is like a giant funnel. It has a wide opening at one end, with lots of potential customers coming in. The opening at the other end, where paying customers come out, is much narrower. Only a fraction of the people who enter the funnel pass all the way through. The more people you get into your funnel, and the more of them you bring through to the other side, the more money you'll make.

There are four yes-or-no decisions that each potential customer will make as he or she travels through your funnel. These decision points narrow the funnel and bring the right people closer to the other side.

Decision #1: Do they want to visit your website? This decision actually takes place outside of your funnel, on the internet—all 20 billion pages of it. Millions of people are out there, doing searches, looking at ads and reading content on other sites. Some of those people will see your ad or a link to your website and click on it. At that moment of the mouse click, an internet user enters your sales funnel and becomes your website visitor.

Decision #2: Do they want to hear what you have to say? "Website visitors" are just people who open a page on your website. They may have gotten there by accident or because they're looking for a certain type of business or because they're looking specifically for you or your company. You don't know much about them at this point, and they don't know much about you.

Some of your visitors will "bounce" and disappear right away. If you've done a good job designing your site, this will only happen to visitors who shouldn't have been there in the first place—people who clicked on the wrong link or used the wrong words in their internet search.

The visitors who stay on your site are the ones who are looking for the information you're selling. If they stay on your site for more than seven seconds, you can assume they're interested. Those visitors are your sales prospects.

Decision #3: Do they want to introduce themselves? The real moment of truth comes after your sales prospects have read through the introductory information on your website. Have they lost interest, or are they ready to take the next step?

Your goal at this point is to get the sales prospect to express his or her interest to you. The best way to make that happen is to use a "landing page."

A landing page is a specialized page that welcomes first-time visitors to your website. It's not a sales page, and it's not a homepage. It presents a simple yes-or-no question to your sales prospects: Will they "opt in" and provide their contact information in return for a free offer?

If the answer is no, your prospect is not interested in doing business with you. If the answer is yes, you've started a relationship, and your sales prospect has become a sales lead.

We talk about landing pages in detail in Chapter 4.

Decision #4: Do they want to make a purchase? Once your sales leads introduce themselves by opting in on your landing page, it's time to start selling to them. This is the final yes-or-no decision in your sales funnel: Is your sales lead willing to buy your product or service?

Your lead might make a purchase within seconds, or it might take weeks or months for you to close the sale. It all depends on what you're selling and how you sell it. We cover the different ways to use your website as a sales tool in Chapter 5.

What Do You Want From Your Website?

What do you want from your website? It's a simple question, but we've found that many business owners can't answer it. They know websites are supposed to be good for business, so they build websites, but they never stop to think about the results they're trying to achieve. Often, they end up spending time and money on a site that doesn't do them any good at all.

Once you know what your sales funnel looks like, you'll answer that question for yourself. The answer will guide you through the process of building, promoting and improving your site.

Sales on Your Website vs. Sales From Your Website

The ultimate goal of any business website is to generate sales. There are two ways of using a website to do that: You can generate sales *on* your website, or you can generate sales *from* your website.

When you generate sales *on* your website, your website is your entire sales funnel. The sales process takes place online from start to finish.

In this business model, your website is essentially an online store. It presents your list of products and prices, takes orders, processes payments and provides shipping information (or the product itself, if it's in electronic format such as an e-book or audio file). In most cases, with an online store, you expect visitors to make a purchase on their first visit or after a few visits.

When you generate sales *from* your website, you're not expecting visitors to make a purchase online, at least not on their first few visits. Instead, you use your website as a source of sales leads, and you follow up those leads in the way that makes the most sense for your product or service—by e-mail, fax, phone, mail or even in person.

In this model, your website is only the wide end of your funnel—the piece that brings in potential customers and gets them moving in the right direction. Your other sales tools act as the narrower parts of the funnel and close your sales.

We advise most of our clients to adopt the second model and use their websites as tools to generate leads. You can only expect to close sales online if you're selling low-priced products with a short buying cycle. If your products cost thousands of dollars, if customers need to collect a large amount of information before they make a purchase or if you're selling services, you'll have limited success closing sales on your website.

> If you'd like Bob Regnerus to personally "audit" or critique your landing pages, website or sales funnel, watch his free video at **www.Traffic andSalesMaximizerAudit.com**.

The strategies you learn in this book will help you build an effective website, whether you use it as an online store or as a tool to generate leads. The most important thing is that you know—before you start building your site—which type of site you need and how your site fits with the rest of your business.

Map It Out

The best way to plan your website is to diagram the steps your visitors will take as they move through your sales funnel. Draw a flowchart like the sample presented here. If you're building your website from scratch, draw the process you plan to use. If you have a website already, put yourself in the shoes of a first-time visitor and spend a few minutes clicking through the links on your site. Each time your website asks you to make a decision, add it to your diagram.

If you can describe each step in the process with a simple yes-or-no decision on your flowchart, you're planning a website that will harness the Power of ONE. If you find yourself drawing anything that looks like a wishbone, pitchfork or octopus, you're probably giving your visitors too many choices at once.

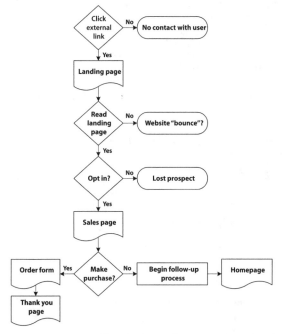

FIGURE 2-3. As you can see, the process of generating a lead is a series of single yes-or-no questions. Drawing your process in this format will help you understand the steps you need to take your prospect from casual visitor to customer.

Landing Page vs. Homepage

You probably noticed that the "homepage" is the final step in the sample flowchart. This may seem odd to you at first because you're probably used to thinking of a homepage as the first stop on any website visit. In reality, it's the last place you want to send one of your potential customers.

We're not saying that your website shouldn't have a homepage. A homepage has many uses for many types of visitors, but that's exactly why you shouldn't use it to greet first-time visitors. It can't do a good job of guiding people through your sales funnel because it has too many other jobs to do. Our focus in this book is on the pages of your website that play an active part in converting visitors into customers.

> For more internet information marketing funnel process examples, visit **InternetInfoMarketingBook.com/funnels**.

The Power of ONE in Action

In February 2008, Barack Obama set a new record for political fundraising. He pulled in $55 million that month, $20 million more than his rival, Hillary Clinton, raised over the same period. At the time, the two candidates were within a percentage point or two of each other in the polls, so Senator Obama didn't raise more money because he had more supporters.

What made such a difference, then? We're not going to say we can explain the entire $20 million, but we suspect that a large part of it had to do with the websites the candidates were using that month. After all, over $45 million of Obama's $55 million was donated online.

Take a look at the screenshot of Senator Clinton's site. This is the front page of **HillaryClinton.com** as of February 2008 (Figure 2-4).

In terms of layout and design, Senator Clinton's website was

FIGURE 2-4. A screen-capture image of Hillary Clinton's campaign website in the 2008 Democratic presidential race—what's the objective of this website?

virtually identical to the site Howard Dean used in 2004, when he was the superstar of online fund-raising. It was a typical information portal page, with lots of links, menus and different types of content. This might have been OK for people who had been to the site many times and wanted to browse.

However, if you were only interested in donating to the campaign and saw this page for the first time, you'd have to spend some time looking for the right way to do it. If you weren't a die-hard Clinton supporter, you might lose interest and click away, or you might get distracted by one of the other links on the page, read for a while and then leave, having never made that contribution.

Now, look at the front page of **BarackObama.com** as of February 2008.

FIGURE 2-5. A screen-capture image of Barack Obama's campaign website in the 2008 Democratic presidential race—using the Power of ONE to raise more money.

Senator Obama used a more modern approach to his website: an approach that harnessed the Power of ONE. His front page was basically a landing page. It presented one yes-or-no decision and a simple call to action: "Make a Donation." And as we know, that's what a record number of people did.

Of course, Senator Obama had to offer other links and content on his site, and he used a page that looked similar to the Clinton front page to do that. The difference was that visitors didn't see that page until they'd seen the landing page. By eliminating distractions and asking visitors to make a simple yes-or-no decision, Senator Obama maximized his chances of collecting campaign contributions on his website.

This isn't a book on political science, so we're not going to guess at any of the other things that may have helped Senator Obama that February. The point here is that these two websites were in direct competition, and one of them generated 57 percent more income, even though the two candidates had the same amount of political support. It was no coincidence, if you ask us, that more money flowed into the website that harnessed the Power of ONE.

Info-Marketer Profile

Melanie Benson Strick Engineers Success for Business Owners

Melanie Benson Strick is an engineer of sorts. Not the bridge-building, factory-optimizing or development-planning kind, but an engineer nonetheless. She identifies where her clients want to go and then designs a process to get them there.

Her 10 years with Motorola showed Melanie that she had a special knack of bringing people together to solve problems. "I started in a beginning role of helping out with getting trade shows organized for state and local governments as well as the trucking and gaming industries—organizations filled with people who needed Motorola's two-way communications," she says. "I would work with mayors and fire departments and industry leaders to determine the kind of support we needed to give them. It was a lot of fun."

Melanie's trade show experience evolved into taking on projects involving technology. She worked as a go-between for customers and various departments at Motorola to establish 9-1-1 call centers. "It was really fascinating from the team approach," Melanie recalls, "because I learned very early on how to get the different factions of Motorola to work together to solve our clients' problems. But I

➡

didn't like the technology, so I began looking for ways to have more fun and do the part I like, which is helping clients get to a result on time. You could say I 'reverse engineered' a process by saying 'this is where the client wants to be; how do we get there? How do we solve the problems that are in the way?' That led me to what I'm doing today."

But it was a rocky road for Melanie when she left Motorola. She didn't know much about how to use the internet to attract clients, and just two weeks after she went out on her own in late 2001, the 9/11 terrorist attacks left the entire country reeling. "I thought I was going to do lifestyle coaching for corporate employees who were struggling to find themselves, but after 9/11, the marketplace disintegrated," she says. "It was pretty naive of me to think I could just go out and become a coach. I didn't know how to pull it together."

Melanie's struggles continued for 2½ years. "From the sheer necessity of being almost bankrupt, completely broke and having absolutely no idea how to get clients to come to me, I started going to seminars," she says, "and I saw Alexandria Brown speak one day."

Melanie hired Ali to help her transform her business. The first thing that needed to change was Melanie's website. Ali showed her that a beautifully designed website with eye-catching graphics was a waste of space on the internet. "Ali kind of slapped my wrist and said, 'What the heck is this graphic site you have online that's doing nothing?'" Melanie laughs.

Melanie rebuilt her website, adding a landing page that invited visitors to leave their e-mail addresses in exchange for a free report, "Five Massive Mistakes That Can Put You Out of Business and How to Avoid Them." The report included a CD, a subscription to her e-zine, *The Success Connection,* and an assessment of where the potential client was in developing his or her business. Melanie used this

➡

free report to connect with people about the pain they were experiencing in trying to build their own businesses. She included stories about other people and how she solved their problems. "Instead of just saying, 'Here's the problem. Here's what I do to solve it,' I tell great stories about somebody who was overwhelmed and how I helped them develop a crystal-clear plan of action," Melanie explains. "I help them to see that they are victims of what I call the 'Bright Shiny Object Syndrome.' When you're chasing a new, bright, shiny object every day, you're going to be overwhelmed. When I tell them I have a formula to break free of that syndrome, potential clients get curious and want to go to the next step with me."

In the beginning, Melanie tried a relatively high price point for people to get her life coaching advice. "I told potential clients that for $350 or $500 a month, I could help them solve their problems. It was just very unrealistic for many people to take a jump that quickly at that price point. So, one of the things I did was to develop different levels at which people could access my information."

For example, Melanie offers a "Get Out of Overwhelm" CD and guidebook for $47, and her entry-level "The Ultimate Wealth and Success Circle" coaching program is $97 a month. She also has a midlevel coaching program offered at $297 for a 6-month commitment, as well as a 12-month platinum coaching group that goes for $1,250 per month. By inviting people in at all different levels, Melanie maximizes her conversion of prospects into mentoring clients.

To keep things interesting and to build her list, Melanie makes special offers around holidays or special events. "One of the most successful things I ever did was built around my Caribbean vacation to St. John one November," Melanie says. "My team put together a campaign that said, 'She's gone. We finally got rid of her. She needed a vacation, and to celebrate, we want to help you get ➡

out of overwhelm and start living the lifestyle you've always dreamed of with this special on the "Get Out of Overwhelm" CD.' We ran a special for $9.95, and we sold around 250 of those CDs. That CD was an effective hook to get them to ask about coaching with me."

One of the secrets to Melanie's success is her love of collaboration. "I'm not really too excited about doing things on my own," she laughs. "I'm much better as a collaborator. I love partnering with other people to leverage their brilliance." Melanie partners with another coach who, like her, came out of the corporate marketplace. "Shawn Driscoll is super strong in terms of systems and process, so we have co-created the curriculum and videos for my coaching programs."

Chapter 3

The Five Kings of Internet Information Marketing

I F YOU EXAMINE HISTORY, YOU'LL FIND FEW EXAMPLES OF KINGS WHO shared a crown. Charlemagne shared France with his brother for a year or two, but the brother died under mysterious circumstances. In ancient Rome, Crassus and Pompey ruled the empire along with Julius Caesar until Caesar started a war and put an end to the arrangement. Sharing power just isn't something kings like to do.

You may be skeptical, then, when we tell you about a kingdom that has five kings. The Five Kings of this kingdom have ruled together for many years, and they don't plot against each other or build up separate armies. In fact, the kings only have a kingdom to rule because they work together.

Who are the Five Kings? Their names are King Salutation, King Presentation, King Consummation, King Perseverance and King Enticement. Their kingdom is surrounded on all sides by an enormous wilderness in which other kingdoms are constantly rising and falling. The wilderness is filled with wanderers, each of whom is on a separate quest. Those wanderers are the reason for the kingdom's survival.

Each time a wanderer enters the kingdom and completes a quest, he or she leaves behind a few gold coins. The more people who visit the kingdom, the richer the kingdom becomes.

So, to maintain their kingdom, the Five Kings must guide wanderers into the land and guide them through to the completion of their quests. In this effort, each king has a specific job to do. If one of them ignores his duty or tries to do another king's work instead of his own, he jeopardizes the future of the entire kingdom. On the other hand, when the Five Kings join forces and coordinate their efforts, their treasure chests overflow with gold and jewels. Let's take a closer look at these Five Kings and how they work together.

King Salutation

King Salutation is in charge of welcoming visitors in from the wilderness. He and his knights stand at the gates at the border of the kingdom, greeting everyone who approaches. People come to the kingdom in many ways, from many directions, and King Salutation must give an appropriate greeting to each. He must be able to recognize what each visitor is looking for, and he must say the right things to bring the visitor through the gates.

King Salutation has a genius for making people feel comfortable, which aids him in his work. He doesn't frighten people away by asking too many questions or by trying to rush them inside. He gives each visitor a warm welcome, introduces himself and describes his kingdom with a few choice words. He doesn't force his visitors to listen to the entire history of the kingdom, nor does he burden them with unnecessary details. He knows that many of his visitors have doubts and questions, and he offers them answers and encouragement.

The king recognizes that each wanderer who comes to the gate is on a quest and is anxious to complete it. Most visitors come to the kingdom because they were sent by another king, King Enticement, but some have arrived by accident. King Salutation describes his kingdom accurately to everyone, so that visitors who are on a different quest can be on their way without wasting time.

If a visitor's quest can be completed in the kingdom, King Salutation invites the visitor to pass beyond the border. To encourage his visitors, King Salutation offers each one a small gift and asks only for the visitor's name in return.

King Presentation

King Presentation is the kingdom's official tour guide. He specializes in convincing visitors that their quests can be completed within the kingdom. When a visitor gives his name to King Salutation and passes through the gates, King Presentation is there on the other side, ready to lead the visitor through the kingdom.

King Presentation is a masterful speaker. He captures the imagination of his visitors and opens their eyes to the wonders of his kingdom. He knows, as do all the kings, that his visitors are searching for something. However, some of these wanderers don't know exactly what they're looking for. King Presentation knows how to point these uncertain travelers in the right direction. They can wander in the wilderness for years, he tells them, or they can achieve their goals right here in the kingdom.

Many visitors, when they arrive in the kingdom, are afraid that they'll leave their gold behind and still have to continue on their quest. King Presentation helps them overcome their fears by telling stories of wanderers who came before them and of the quests that have been completed within the kingdom.

This king knows how to get the attention of a sleepy wanderer, and he knows how to make complicated ideas appear simple. When a visitor seems to lack motivation, the king spurs him or her to action with additional small gifts and eloquent speeches.

King Consummation

After King Presentation has energized and inspired the kingdom's visitors, King Consummation tells the visitors what they must do next. He overcomes any final fears or objections the visitors might have, and he shows them how to exchange their gold for the objects they seek.

Of the Five Kings, King Consummation is the least visible. He stays close to the special places in the kingdom where quests can be completed. He does not make his presence known to the general public, and he prefers to meet with wanderers only after they have met with King Salutation and King Presentation.

It doesn't always work out that way, however. Some visitors to the kingdom don't want to take the time to meet with King Presentation, so they rush past him and seek out King Consummation instead. Some of these visitors scale the walls of the kingdom, passing up King Salutation as well. They do this for one of two reasons. Either they know exactly what they want and can't wait to get it, or they want to find out if the completion of their quests will require too much of them.

In either case, King Consummation must be prepared. He helps the eager travelers as quickly as possible, guiding them through before they lose heart. He deals gently with the nervous ones, reassuring them they will gain more than they give up.

No matter how visitors come to King Consummation, his job is the same: to provide all the information the visitors need before they take the final steps of their journeys. Even though the visitors have traveled a long way already, many of them aren't certain that they want to continue. King Consummation knows that different people hesitate for different reasons, and his goal is to address every concern that a traveler might have. He uses many of the same techniques used by King Salutation and King Presentation, and he offers to protect visitors in the unlikely event they are unhappy with the conclusion of their visits.

King Perseverance

King Perseverance has the least glamorous job of the Five Kings, but he brings in as much wealth as the other four combined. He is the king responsible for maintaining a relationship with visitors who leave the kingdom before they complete their quests. This is more important than it might sound. Despite the best efforts of King Salutation, King Presentation and King Consummation, most visitors leave the kingdom soon after they enter. If it were not for King Perseverance, those visitors would be lost to the kingdom forever.

King Salutation, as you now know, asks each visitor to leave his or her name before entering the kingdom. This is not a matter of security. King Salutation collects those names so that King Perseverance can do his job.

With the list of names he gets from King Salutation, King Perseverance and his knights follow visitors through the wilderness and encourage them to return to the kingdom. Some of those visitors return as soon as they're asked, and others are slow to respond. King Perseverance knows how to persist without being a nuisance, and he often contacts wanderers seven times or more before he succeeds in convincing them to make another visit to the kingdom.

With so many wanderers to follow and so many messages to deliver, King Perseverance needs more assistance than the other kings. He employs a special army of couriers who deliver messages to wanderers in every part of the wilderness. These messages are delivered frequently, sometimes once a day. The travelers who receive them feel as though they are communicating with the king himself, and many of them return to the kingdom to complete their quests.

King Enticement

King Enticement rules from afar. In fact, he never sets foot on his own land. He spends his time in the surrounding wilderness, asking strangers to journey to his kingdom. That might sound easy at first because the wilderness is full of people, but King Enticement does more than sit on his horse and shout at everyone who passes by. He might send more visitors to the kingdom that way, but most of those visitors would do more harm than good. They'd consume resources, block the roads and contribute nothing in return. The king is looking for specific types of visitors, and to find them, he has to know the places where those people are likely to be.

In a way, King Enticement has the most difficult job of all, but he has one thing working in his favor: Many people in the wilderness are looking for him at the same time. No one in the wilderness stays in one place for long, and everyone out there is looking for something. King Enticement's kingdom is where the lucky ones can complete their quests. They don't know about the kingdom, though, so they wander through the forests, deserts and swamps, looking for someone to show them the way.

The king has plenty of help out there in the wilderness. In addition to his own knights, he hires agents and ambassadors. His agents search the more remote areas of the wilderness, looking for wanderers the king himself would not be able to reach. His ambassadors travel to faraway kingdoms and send the people from those kingdoms to visit King Salutation, King Presentation and the rest, in return for a few pieces of silver.

How You Can Become a King of the Internet

The story of the Five Kings is not a fairy tale. As you've probably guessed, it's a parable about marketing on the internet. The Five Kings' kingdom is actually a website, and the surrounding wilderness is the rest of the internet. Every wanderer who passes through the kingdom on a quest is a potential customer. The Five Kings, who guide wanderers in from the wilderness and through the kingdom to the completion of their quests, represent the five steps of the marketing process.

Just as all Five Kings need to work together without getting in each other's way, you need to include all five steps in your marketing campaign, and you need to follow these steps in their proper order.

If you want to test out how effective your sales funnel is, have it critiqued by Bob Regnerus personally! Visit **TrafficandSalesMaximizer Audit.com** for more information.

Step 1: Establishing a Relationship

Before you start selling, you have to establish a relationship with your website visitor. You do that in the same way you establish any other relationship: by welcoming your visitor and asking for his or her name. King Salutation does this job for his kingdom, and your landing page does it for your website.

We mentioned landing pages briefly in Chapter 2 because they help you harness the Power of ONE. They simplify the experience for your customers, and they let you control the information your customers see. They also establish your credibility, lay the foundation for your sales process and enhance your future marketing campaigns.

An effective landing page uses a bold headline to capture the visitor's attention and then presents an offer to the visitor. The offer can be a free report, a sample product or anything else the visitor will find appealing. In return for the offer, the landing page asks the visitor to "opt in" and provide an e-mail address or other contact information.

It's important to remember that a landing page is not a sales page. It should simply get your visitors' attention, make them feel comfortable and present an offer. By giving visitors the choice to opt in or opt out, you'll build your contact list and focus your sales efforts on people who have already expressed an interest.

We take a detailed look at landing pages, including the eight elements that every landing page should include, in Chapter 4.

Step 2: Converting Visitors Into Customers

After a visitor opts in on your landing page, the selling process begins. If you want to be successful, your sales materials must have the qualities embodied by King Presentation: They must be engaging, informative and inspiring. The material must also be delivered in a way that maximizes your chances of making a sale.

There are three basic models for making a sales presentation to a website visitor:

Sales Model #1: The online sales presentation. This is often the simplest model to use, so it's the model many information marketers adopt when they're getting started in the business. After a visitor opts in on your landing page, he or she is taken to a sales page. The sales page uses compelling copy, multimedia content and customer testimonials to convert the visitor into a customer.

Sales Model #2: The tele-seminar. A tele-seminar is a sales presentation delivered over the phone. If you follow this model, your landing page will offer participation in the seminar in exchange for the visitor's e-mail address or other contact information. After the visitor opts in, a page should open that provides all the details about the seminar.

Sales Model #3: The "Shock-and-Awe" package. Dan Kennedy pioneered the use of the "Shock-and-Awe" package, which is a box of sales materials in multiple formats, delivered to the sales lead's home. This is a great tool if you're selling higher-priced products or services.

In Chapter 5, we see these models in action, and we talk about the five things every sales presentation should do, no matter which delivery method you choose.

Step 3: Asking for the Sale

King Consummation is the king who gives visitors step-by-step instructions on how to complete their quests. In your internet marketing campaign, this is the job of your order form.

Many business owners, even those with good landing pages and good sales presentations, treat their order forms as an afterthought. This is a mistake. No matter how good your sales materials are, many of your potential customers will still be undecided when they look at your order form. If you use a generic, uninformative or poorly designed form, you're almost certain to lose those undecided customers.

There's another reason to put some effort into your order form. Remember the wanderers who ignore King Salutation and King Presentation and rush straight to King Consummation? Those are the internet users who skip past your sales presentation, and maybe even your landing page, to get a look at your order form. Some of them have already decided to buy and don't need to be convinced. Others want to see what your product or service will cost before they spend any time reading, watching or listening to your sales presentation. If you provide the key points and arguments from your sales presentation, you may be able to convert visitors directly on your order form. Chapter 6 tells you everything you need to know about the ordering process, including the seven things every order form needs to do.

Step 4: Following Up

Even if you do everything right on your landing page, your sales presentation and your order form, most of your first-time website visitors will leave your site without buying anything. If you want another chance to sell to those visitors, you must follow the example of King Perseverance. An automated follow-up e-mail campaign will bring many of your unconverted leads back for additional visits—you may increase your sales by 100 percent or more!

Your follow-up campaign actually begins on your landing page. Without the list of addresses you collect on your landing page, you would have no way of knowing about a visitor who was interested in your product or service, but wasn't ready to make a purchase. By getting visitors to opt in and provide their e-mail addresses, you set yourself up for a second opportunity.

We recommend that our clients send their sales leads at least seven e-mails over a two-week period, starting with the lead's first visit to the website. The e-mails should be short, informative and personalized. Each e-mail should invite the recipient to return to the website.

Sending seven personalized e-mails to every sales lead would require an office full of people if it weren't for the magic of the autoresponder. An autoresponder is a program that sends e-mails for you, using the list from your landing page. Just as King Perseverance uses an army of couriers to send his messages throughout the wilderness, you can use an autoresponder to send dozens of e-mails every day without lifting a finger. We talk more about autoresponders and follow-up campaigns in Chapter 7.

Step 5: Generating the Right Traffic

King Enticement, the king who never visits his kingdom, plays his part by sending wanderers in from the wilderness. The prosperity of the kingdom depends on a steady flow of motivated visitors whose quests can be completed with the help of King Salutation, King Presentation and King Consummation.

In the same way, the success of your business depends on a steady flow of interested consumers to your website. The more traffic you generate to your site, the more chances you have to make sales.

That's not all there is to it, though. Getting more traffic is not enough. You have to get the right type of traffic. If you bring in thousands of visitors who aren't interested in your product, you'll accomplish nothing. The answer is targeted traffic—traffic made up of consumers who are likely to buy what you're selling.

There are dozens of ways to generate targeted traffic, but they fall into two main categories: You can pay for it, or you can generate it organically. Paid traffic comes from advertisements, affiliate programs and sponsorships, among other sources. Organic traffic comes from search engine results, web directories, links on other websites and often from your existing customers. Chapter 8 gives you step-by-step instructions for generating targeted traffic for your website.

> To make your sales presentation more powerful, you have to be different! To help you stand out in crowd, read the free bonus chapter at **InternetInfo MarketingBook.com/usp**.

It's Time to Roll Up Your Sleeves

In these first three chapters, we've been looking at the big picture. In Chapter 1, you saw why the internet is such a valuable resource for information marketers, and you discovered the new opportunities the internet has made available. In Chapter 2, you learned the fundamental concepts and strategies that will guide you in all of your internet marketing efforts.

Here in Chapter 3, you met the Kings of Internet Marketing, each of whom plays a role in an effective internet marketing campaign. The kings have years of experience and a long history of success. In the next five chapters, they tell you everything they know. Once you've learned the secrets of the Five Kings, you'll be ready to lead your own kingdom to happiness and prosperity.

Info-Marketer Profile

How Yanik Silver Mastered the Art of Sales at Age 14 and Went On to Become an Internet Marketing Guru

Yanik Silver took to information marketing naturally; he grew up in an entrepreneurial family.

"We're a family of Russian immigrants," Yanik explains. "We came to the United States when I was 2½ years old, and my dad was fired from his first job because he refused to stop moonlighting." ➡

The elder Silver supplemented his family's income by repairing medical equipment for doctors. Given an ultimatum to stop moonlighting or be let go, he decided to open his own medical equipment repair and sales business. "Growing up in a business like that, you pretty much do whatever you need to do in a family business," Yanik says. "By the age of 14, I was doing telemarketing, getting all my own leads, and then following up on those leads and making sales. By age 16, I was on the road cold-calling on doctors. So, I learned sales skills really early on."

With his early start in sales, Yanik was ready to jump into direct marketing as soon as he heard about it … at the ripe old age of 17. "One of my doctor customers gave me a Jay Abraham tape. It was amazing! I couldn't believe that by using direct marketing you could get people to give you money without you being there in person. The light went on, and I started devouring every single possible resource I could find and afford (or not afford, really)."

Yanik ordered products from Dan Kennedy, Ted Nicholas and "all of the old greats," as he puts it. Then he started writing ads using Joe Sugarman's long form style. Those ads led to good leads, and soon Yanik was making sales. That's when he started consulting with some of his doctor clients, teaching them how to do the kind of marketing he was doing.

It wasn't long before Yanik realized there were more doctors who could use the kind of information he had, so he created a box of materials following the Jeff Paul model. "It was really exciting to be selling a high-priced box to a niche, and I picked dermatologists as my first niche," Yanik remembers. "I wrote an ad for a dermatologic surgery publication. I don't remember how much it cost, but it was a little classified ad. I got 10 leads from it."

At first those leads went nowhere. Yanik sent his free report to those 10 leads, but nothing happened. He sent a second notice. ➡

Still nothing.

"I remember calling Heather Krueger. She worked for Jeff Paul," Yanik says. "I told her I didn't know what to do, and she said, 'Oh, honey, just send out the third notice.' Well, I followed her advice, and on the last day of the deadline, there it was: a fax with my first order for $500!"

Then the work began. Yanik needed a product—fast.

"After I got over the joy and excitement of seeing that first order come in, I realized I had to produce the darn thing," Yanik laughs. "So, I wrote the doctor and told him the manual was being republished and I wouldn't charge his card until it was available. I basically worked nonstop for a couple of weeks, staying up till three or four in the morning to get that thing finished and out there."

Building on his success with the dermatology niche, Yanik soon expanded into other niches, including cosmetic surgeons and LASIK (eye surgery) surgeons. But the biggest expansion was yet to come.

In late 1999, Yanik started looking at the possibilities of using the internet for direct marketing. "I saw people selling e-books, and they were just one long sales letter," he says. "I thought about all the great advantages of the internet, like speed of delivery, no cost of delivery or service, and you could literally put up a site for a couple hundred bucks."

Yanik was especially intrigued by models being used by Kenny Voy and Marlin Sanders. "Their companies were affiliate-driven, and I decided that's where I was going to focus once I had a successful product."

He didn't plan it, but it was probably inevitable: Yanik Silver became a bona fide internet marketing guru. What else would you expect from someone who had mastered the art of telemarketing and direct sales by age 14?

Yanik created his product by asking himself questions. "It's the questions you pose to yourself that create the answers," he explains. "I asked myself, 'How can I create a fully automatic money-making website that makes me money while I sleep and provides an incredible value to people instead of just an e-book?'"

The answer came to him in his sleep.

Yanik remembers, "I literally woke up at 3 in the morning. I started poking my wife saying, 'Fast, fast, get up, this is going to be good, instant sales letters!' Well, she knows how it is with entrepreneurs; they always have lots of ideas, so she says, 'Yeah, go back to sleep.' But I knew this one was gonna be good, so I jumped out of bed and registered that domain name. I started working on it the next day."

It took a month for Yanik to get his product up and running, and then the orders started coming in: "We made $1,800 my first month, $3,600 the second month, then $7,800 the next month and then $9,200—that's when people really started paying attention to what I was doing, how I kind of burst on the scene so quickly and had a six-figure website."

So Yanik was an "overnight success," but not really. "I don't really believe in overnight successes," he says, "because if you go back and look at my career, I started studying direct response in 1997. The website came out in 2000, so I had several years of learning the fundamentals of direct response. I'm a big student of the masters of copywriting, of mail order, of direct response, and I think all of those fundamentals played a key factor in my success online."

Yanik credits Earl Nightingale for helping him succeed: "Really early on I took it close to heart where he talks about if you want to become an expert in a subject, read for one hour a night for three years. If you want to become a world expert, read for one hour a night for five years. And I thought, well, what would happen if you read and studied for two hours a night or three hours a night?"

You become an expert, and that leads to success. That's what happens.

Today, Yanik has 25 websites and products in five marketplaces. That might make you wonder how he gets everything done. Leverage is Yanik's secret to time management.

He explains, "I've always tried to think about how I can leverage my activities. If I'm going to do an interview, I transcribe it at the same time and turn it into a multipart autoresponder. That way, it goes out as a follow-up to people after they've gotten on my list. Or if I write an article, I'll put that in the autoresponder sequence. I also focus on evergreen, fundamental stuff rather than the newest, most cutting-edge things. In the internet world, it's really easy to get focused on what's the newest, coolest tool or the newest, coolest thing. But if you're doing that, then you've got a content problem because you constantly have to reinvent and recreate everything."

In addition to leveraging his time by making one activity do multiple things, Yanik focuses his time on the parts of his business that yield the best results for him. "Some niches do better than others," Yanik shrugs, "so I'm going to spend more time creating promotions for those than for the other ones."

Yanik hosts one large seminar each year, "The Underground Online Seminar" (**UndergroundOnlineSeminar.com**). He also does coaching "sort of," as he puts it.

Sticking to his practice of both leveraging and focusing his time, Yanik has reduced the amount of time he spends on coaching. "My big push this year is the site **InternetLifestyle.com**," he says. "It's a combination of making a whole lot of money and also living a good, balanced life with family and having a lot of fun, not just being 99 percent focused on work and making more money and all that."

➡

Yanik is a believer in the 80/20 rule: "You know that 20 percent of your work creates 80 percent of your profits, and 20 percent of your clients create 80 percent of your problems. I constantly work to focus on the things that create the most profit and set up the rest of my business to automate the functions that don't produce profits." He puts his personal efforts into running two mastermind groups and his annual seminar, selling DVDs of his seminar and producing his $87-per-month newsletter. "With just those three items that I spend some time on and then all the automated stuff, it's very easy for me to get into seven figures without pushing myself and having to be completely focused on work," Yanik says.

Another way Yanik leverages his time is by focusing on the things he's good at and contracting out the things that he's not. Even though he's considered an internet marketing guru, Yanik says he is "totally nontechnical."

"A lot of people get hung up on this. They think if they're going to start an internet business or add an internet facet to their business, they have to be some techno whiz, and they need to build the pages themselves, or they must really know about technology," Yanik says. "The truth is, I call myself a 'techno dunce.' I still have no idea how to put up a website—I never have, and I don't know if I ever will because that's a $50-per-hour activity I can get someone else to do for me. I would much rather be focusing on $1,000-per-hour activities."

Yanik is quick to stress that everyone has unique abilities to do certain things, and so he does the things he excels at and seeks out other skilled people to do the things he can't do or doesn't want to do. "You can hire expertise and skill," he says. "I can write a headline or work up an e-mail teaser in my sleep, but for other things, I've been focusing on adding people who have unique abilities in other areas. Graphics, for instance. I had this really cool logo designed ➡

for me for **InternetLifestyle.com**. I think it's a great logo, and there's no way I could have created this thing, but for the person who did, I'm sure it felt easy. For any obstacle you can think of in the information marketing world, there's somebody else who can do it for you, and it's easy for them."

Chapter 4

King
Salutation

Establishing a Relationship With Your Customer

ING SALUTATION GETS OUR VOTE AS THE MOST IMPORTANT OF the Five Kings. He absolutely must do a good job of welcoming visitors to the kingdom—that's what makes King Enticement's efforts pay off and gives King Presentation, King Consummation and King Perseverance a chance to do their work.

King Salutation's domain—your landing page—is the single most important element of your internet marketing campaign. Your landing page is where you ask visitors to take the first step toward becoming customers. If a visitor says yes, your sales, ordering and follow-up systems all swing into action. If a visitor says no, you've lost your chance with him or her, probably forever.

In this chapter, we're going to take a detailed look at what a landing page can do for your website and what you need to include on your landing page to ensure that it works.

What Is a Landing Page?

We've mentioned landing pages a few times already, but let's start with the basics. A landing page is not a sales page, an order form, an information portal or a homepage. It's a page designed with one goal in mind: to convince visitors to "opt in," or announce their interest in doing business with you. This is the page visitors land on when they come to your site from an external source, such as an advertisement, a search results page or a referral link on another website.

Landing pages are also called squeeze pages, opt-in pages or "shy yes" pages, but whatever you call them, the idea is the same. They are the best way to welcome potential customers to your website, and they allow you to establish the right type of relationship with your visitors.

An effective landing page is simple. It describes your product or service with a bold headline and a short, clear message. It establishes your credibility by displaying customer testimonials and well-written copy. Finally, it asks your visitors to provide information about themselves in return for a free (or very inexpensive) introductory offer. The more visitors you convince to opt in, the more sales you'll make.

Four Reasons You Need a Landing Page

1. It Gets Attention

Too many companies use what we call "brochure websites." Brochure websites provide information, but that's all they do. They don't tailor information to fit the needs of the individual visitor, and they don't ask the visitor to take action. They are definitely not the right solution for any business looking to increase its conversion rate.

A brochure website is limited because it uses a traditional homepage, which treats everyone the same way. Every visitor sees the same thing when they open a brochure-style site, whether the visitor is an employee, a vendor, an existing customer or a potential customer. For employees and vendors, and maybe even for existing customers, a homepage is OK. They've probably been to the site many times before, and even if they haven't, they have a reason to stick around and find what they need.

Potential customers, on the other hand, have no reason to dig through an unhelpful site. Remember what you learned in Chapter 2: You must grab your visitors' attention in the first three to seven seconds of their visit. If you want to get your visitors' attention, keep them on your website and get them to take the first step toward becoming customers, you need to greet them with a landing page.

As we mentioned in Chapter 2, there may be a place in your marketing campaign for a brochure-style site. Among other things, a brochure site can give you a place to host your blog, publish your articles and offer customer service. It just can't do a good job of capturing sales leads, and that's what keeps you in business.

2. It Keeps Things Simple

Since your landing page is designed for potential customers and no one else, you can strip away everything that doesn't speak to their needs. All a potential customer needs to know is what you're selling and whether you can be trusted. A landing page answers those two questions as quickly as possible and then asks the visitor to express his or her interest.

Educational materials, sales presentations and everything else can wait until later. Your visitors want to take small steps at first, and they'll reward you for keeping things simple.

3. It Lets You Build Your List

The information you collect on your landing page is valuable. Whether you're collecting e-mail addresses or full contact information (name, street address, phone number), you're building a list you can use in your current marketing campaign and in every future campaign you develop. If you use a brochure-style website, you'll never have that opportunity because you're not taking steps to identify people who are interested in your product or service.

4. It Gives You What You Really Need

Most businesses, including most information marketers, should not expect a website visitor to make a purchase on his or her first visit. In most cases, the best use of a website is developing sales leads. Once your visitors have accepted your offer and submitted their contact information, you can start selling to them through any medium you choose: e-mail, telephone, direct mail or even in person.

A sales website can only support an online merchant—a website that makes sales right there on the page. Generally, that sales model works only for lower-priced products or for services with short buying cycles.

If you're unsure how to build a landing page or would rather outsource the whole process to designers who have been hand-trained by Bob Regnerus on creating sites that sell, visit **SalesMaximizerWebsite.com**.

A lead-generating website, on the other hand, can support every type of business. By using a landing page to identify potential customers and collect their contact information, you take full advantage of your website.

The Eight Essential Elements of Your Landing Page

As you learned in Chapter 2, you need to plan your website before you start building it. You have to know how your website fits into your business as a whole, and you have to know what type of output you expect to get from the site. Once you've answered those questions, it's time to start planning the individual pieces of your site, starting with the landing page.

Your landing page should be tailored to fit your business and product. There's no standard template for landing pages, and you shouldn't try to take a shortcut by imitating other landing pages you've seen. There are, however, eight elements that every landing page needs to include:

- The right domain name
- A clear headline
- Good copy
- An appealing offer
- A call to action
- Credibility
- Multimedia content
- Effective design and layout

After we cover these fundamentals, we look at some additional considerations, such as how to optimize your landing page for Google and what to do with the information your landing page collects.

Your Domain Name

A good internet information marketing campaign starts with a good domain name. A good domain name is one that does more than simply provide the name of your business. It provides basic information about the problem you help your customers solve.

If you're selling information about diabetes control, your domain name should include the word *diabetes* and other relevant words like *info*, *help* or *control*. A domain name based on a company name, your own name or a fanciful play on words won't help visitors figure out what you have to offer. Don't try to be artistic with your domain names—the simpler and more direct, the better.

If you're just getting started in information marketing, picking a domain name is fairly simple. Just figure out what name will best communicate the benefits of your product or service.

If you already have a brochure-style website for your business, this can get complicated because your existing website most likely has one of those general-sounding names. In this case, we recommend using a new domain name for your landing page rather than putting your landing page on your existing site. Of course, you'll want to provide links to your landing page from your existing site, and you may want to direct visitors to your main site after they opt in or view your sales presentation.

Each time you add a new type of product or service or begin a marketing campaign, build a landing page and register a new name for it. You may need to spend some time searching for a good available name, or you may need to spend some extra money buying one that has already been registered, but in either case, the results will justify the expense.

Your Headline

Word for word, your landing page headline is the most important text on your entire website. It determines whether you succeed in capturing your visitors' attention in those critical first three to seven seconds.

Your landing page headline isn't an advertising tag line, it's not the name of your business, it's not "Family Owned Since 1979" and it's not "Welcome to My Website!" It's a few lines that describe the benefits your visitors will enjoy if they do business with you.

A good headline is large, clear and compelling. It should be in the center of the page, near the top, where your visitors' eyes are going to look first. It shouldn't be more than 20 or 30 words long, but it has to do a lot in those 20 or 30 words.

First, it has to tell your visitors what business you're in. Use small words and simple grammar, and relate your headline as closely as possible to the text of your advertisements. You need to convince your visitors right away that you actually provide the product or service they're looking for.

Your headline has to get your visitors excited. You don't have enough space in your headline to describe your offer in detail, but you should at least indicate that you have something they'll want. Use words like *solution* and *answer* to spark your visitors' curiosity.

Immediately below the headline, use a subheadline to expand on the ideas you've already presented. Again, don't get too wordy here. Just provide another sentence or two with additional detail about your business, product or offer. The subheadline serves as a logical bridge between the headline and the main body of your landing page. It also serves as a visual bridge, leading your visitors' eyes down the page to your main message.

Your Copy

Your copy is where you tell your visitors what you have to offer and what they need to do to get it. It can be text, an audio announcement or a video presentation.

You may have a thousand things to say to your potential customers, but your landing page copy isn't the place to say them. You don't want to use this space to talk about the history of your company, your line of products, your employees or your philosophy. Everything on the page should be written (or said) with one goal in mind: getting your visitors to opt in.

The thing to remember is that your visitors are only interested in how *they* can benefit from doing business with you. All they need to know about you is that you can help them solve their problem. However you deliver it, your message should be about what your visitors can gain. Word choice always matters, so use the words *you* and *your* rather than *I*, *we* or *our*.

An effective landing page has good copy, but it doesn't have a lot of copy. You should be able to make your point in a few paragraphs or a few minutes of audio or video.

Your Offer

Your landing page asks visitors to give you something valuable: their contact information. To get that information, you have to offer something valuable in return. The offer you make on your landing page must be good enough to spur your visitors into action, and it should be something that will continue to work for you even after the exchange has been made.

For information marketers, the right offer is usually a small-scale information product—enough to get a visitor's attention and demonstrate your expertise, but not so much that it undercuts your sales by solving the visitor's problem. Here's a list of things you might want to consider offering:

Free reports/white papers. A report on a development in your industry will give your sales leads firsthand evidence of your knowledge and expertise. As with any offer, don't give away the farm by providing your most valuable information in a free report. Offer an overview of a topic or a more detailed look at one piece of the big picture.

E-books. Generally speaking, it's not a good idea to offer a full-length e-book on your landing page. It's just too much material to give someone, and if people decide to read the entire thing before moving on to your sales presentation, you'll slow down your sales process by weeks.

A short e-book, on the other hand, can be effective in establishing your credibility and authority. Writing it might take a little time, but if you're selling more expensive products or services, the book will be worth the effort.

If your actual product is an e-book, you can offer a free copy of the first chapter on your landing page. If you did a good job writing the book, your prospects won't want to put it down, which in this case means they'll need to buy the complete version.

Audio programs. Downloadable audio files help your leads learn more about you when they're in the car, on the train or otherwise away from their computers. An audio recording of a presentation or an interview, assuming it's on a topic that interests your visitors, can be an appealing offer. Even though video files are becoming easier to share and watch, people still appreciate the simplicity and portability of audio recordings.

Offline products. You don't have to deliver your offer electronically. People still like to get things in the mail, so consider offering a DVD, a booklet or another offline product.

The downside of an offline offer is that you'll have to pay for postage or shipping, and your leads will have to wait a few days to receive the package. The upside is that you'll collect your leads' physical mailing addresses and probably even phone numbers, which will be valuable down the road. If your product or service is expensive or has a longer buying cycle, this is probably the way to go.

Newsletters. A subscription to an e-newsletter is a great landing page offer. Your newsletter is really a marketing tool, but if you present it in the right way, your prospects will feel that they're getting something valuable by opting in.

Of course, the newsletter does actually have to provide value to the subscriber in the form of relevant content. Your newsletter articles should be well written and interesting, and they should appear to be more than advertisements for your product or service.

Special access. If you're selling subscriptions to a membership site, you might want to give your potential customers free access to the site for a week. You'll probably want to restrict access to the most valuable areas of the site to paying customers only to ensure that your leads don't get everything they need during their trial period.

Discounts. Everyone likes a discount. If you're using your website to sell products rather than generate sales leads, this is a good way to collect contact information without adding an unnecessary step to the buying process.

Discounts don't work quite as well if your visitors aren't expected to make a purchase right away because a discount on a hypothetical sale has little value. If you're selling something with a longer buying cycle, it's best to offer something your prospects can use immediately, such as a free report or an audio recording.

You'll need to do some thinking, and possibly some research, to come up with the right offer for your landing page. The more familiar you are with your customers' needs and interests, the more successful you'll be at hooking them with your offer.

Always give your offer a sense of urgency by imposing some sort of limit on it. The limit might be a deadline or a maximum number of people who can receive the offer or a combination of the two. Your visitors are more likely to opt in right away if they can't be sure your offer will be available later.

Remember to sell your offer. Here's one last thing to remember: Even though you're not charging anything for your landing page offer, you still have to "sell" it. When you present your offer in a way that makes it seem valuable to your visitors, you give your visitors a reason to provide the contact information you're asking for in return. If you're enthusiastic about the offer, your visitors will get excited about it as well.

Your enthusiasm won't do much good if the offer actually has no value, so don't give away outdated materials, obsolete information or information that has nothing to do with your actual product or service. Your offer should give your leads a taste of what's available and leave them wanting more.

Your Call to Action

Once you've made your offer, it's time to tell your visitors what you want in return. In almost every case, what you should be asking for is contact information. The goal here is to tell your visitors what to do and how to do it, as plainly and simply as possible.

First, you have to decide exactly what you want from your visitors.

If you're selling e-books, reports or membership in an information portal, you may only need to collect your visitors' e-mail addresses.

If you're selling higher-priced items or items with a longer buying cycle, you'll probably want to collect names, addresses and phone numbers.

If you offer a wide variety of products, you may want to ask your visitors to complete a survey so you can approach each sales lead with appropriate sales materials.

You also have to consider the way you close your sales. If your customers typically make purchases over the phone, your landing page might ask visitors to make an inbound call. If you close sales in person, you might use your landing page to set appointments.

Whatever your landing page asks visitors to do, remember what you've learned about the Power of ONE. Take control and guide your potential customers through the process. Give them one set of options and ask for a yes-or-no decision.

Make your call to action as simple as possible. Some of your visitors will be tired, distracted or uncomfortable using a computer, so hold their hands through the opt-in process. Use a big red arrow to point to the form where they should type in their information. Tell them to hit the "Submit" button when they're finished. You won't insult anyone's intelligence by giving detailed instructions, but you'll lose potential customers if you expect everyone to figure things out on their own.

Credibility

Establishing trust is one of the most important steps in convincing people to opt in on your landing page. You have to convince your visitors that you're a legitimate business, that you'll be able to deliver on your promises, and that you won't misuse the information your visitors give you. The trust you build on your landing page will help your visitors respond to your offer and make them more receptive to your sales and marketing efforts.

Most of the people who come to your landing page know nothing about you or your business. They decided to visit your site on the basis of a 10-word advertisement or a few lines on a search results page, and they have no idea what to expect. Most of them will err on the side of caution, and if they see anything suspicious on your site, they'll leave without a second thought.

The first things your visitors see on your landing page should put them at ease. The page should be professional-looking, easy to read and free of distracting images. Your headline and copy should make it clear what business you're in. All the text on the page should use correct grammar, spelling and punctuation.

Once you've overcome your visitors' initial doubts, you still have a long way to go. You have to convince your visitors that your landing page offer can be trusted, and you have to lay the foundation for the larger requests you're going to make in the future. To do the best possible job of establishing trust, your landing page should include the following elements:

Testimonials. Customer testimonials are the best tools for establishing credibility. A few dozen words from a happy customer will do more than a thousand words from you. Tell your best customers that you're building a new website and ask them for a few words of recommendation. Most of them will be happy to do it.

The more testimonials you can get, the better. Even if you already have 20 on the page, the 21st will have an effect, at least for some visitors. Typically, testimonials are located toward the bottom of a landing page or along one side so visitors don't have to read all of them if they don't want to.

Plain-text testimonials are OK, but they're more effective if they're accompanied by a photo of the person who gave the testimonial—a photo helps convince your visitors the testimonial came from a real person. Video testimonials are even more effective.

Endorsements. An endorsement from an industry expert is almost as good as a customer testimonial. If you can get an endorsement from someone your customers already know and trust, you'll have an easier time gaining their trust yourself. Go through your address book, pick out the 10 highest-profile names and ask each of those people for an endorsement. You may not get them all, but as with customer testimonials, each one helps.

Don't go overboard here and post endorsements from people with no credentials or experience in your market. If you give your brother-in-law a phony title and pretend he's given you a ringing endorsement, your customers will know something's not right.

Here again, include photos of the people who provide your endorsements, and use video endorsements when possible.

Case studies. Case studies of successful projects you've worked on in the past can do a lot to build your credibility with prospective customers. Not only does a case study let you tell the story of another satisfied customer, it gives you an opportunity to showcase the knowledge and expertise that led to the project's successful outcome.

The problem, however, is that case studies are generally too long to include on a landing page. It's better to provide links to your case studies rather than the studies themselves. This works best when your case studies are linked to your customer testimonials.

For example, if you have a testimonial from Susan Jones, put a link like "Click HERE to find out how we helped Susan" directly below her testimonial. When a visitor clicks the link, the case study should open in a separate window. That way, you provide extra information for the visitors who want it without cluttering your landing page with a lot of additional text.

Certifications and memberships. Are you a member of your local

Better Business Bureau? Have you been certified by a trade organization or guild? Does your website have a seal of approval from TRUSTe or another consumer protection service? If so, make sure your visitors know about it.

If one of these certifications is likely to be important to your potential customers, mention it in your landing page copy. Otherwise, list all your certifications and memberships at the bottom of the page, along with the logos of the relevant institutions.

Contact information. Scam artists try to conceal themselves as much as possible while real businesses publicize their phone numbers and mailing addresses. If you want to reassure your visitors that you're a legitimate business, put your contact information on your landing page. This isn't something most visitors will really stop to think about, but in the back of their minds, they'll make note of your contact info and they'll feel better about doing business with you.

Privacy policy. Privacy is a concern for everyone who uses the internet. Your visitors are on their guard against spam, spyware, viruses and identity theft. To counteract these fears, you need a comprehensive privacy policy, and you need to make the details available on your landing page. Your policy should describe the information you collect and what you do with it as well as the steps you take to protect your visitors' information against theft by other parties.

There's no need to put the full text of your policy on the page, but put a link to it at the bottom of the page—that's where your visitors will look for it. The policy should open in a new window or pop-up so it won't take visitors away from your landing page.

It's a good idea to give a quick reassurance, such as "We will never sell your e-mail address to anyone," when you make your call to action.

The e-mails you send to your mailing list should allow recipients to unsubscribe from the list, and the process to unsubscribe should be fairly simple. Most autoresponder systems will handle this for you. Mention the unsubscribe option in your privacy policy—it's standard stuff these days, but you still need to point it out.

Guarantees. Guarantees help close sales in any situation, but they're essential on a website because many people are still nervous about doing business on the internet.

Even if you're not asking your visitors to make a purchase on your site, they'll want some assurance that they'll be protected when they do buy something from you. Your landing page is not the right place to go into detail about your guarantee, but you should mention that you have one and possibly provide a link to the full text.

Your Multimedia

Multimedia content makes a landing page more engaging and com-pelling. It grabs your visitors' attention and keeps them on the page, and it helps you convince them to opt in. Proceed with caution when adding these elements, and make sure your landing page doesn't get cluttered or confusing.

Images. Include a photo of yourself and photos of the people who provide your testimonials. If your offer is visually exciting, include a photo of it as well. Videos are more effective than still images, so replace your photos with videos when you can.

Video. A two- or three-minute video can dramatically improve your opt-in rate. If you use a video, it should take the place of most of the copy on your landing page. It should welcome your visitors, introduce yourself and your business and then get right to the point: make your offer and give a call to action.

Landing page videos create a personal connection, and they make your call to action more compelling.

> To easily incorporate video into your website, use Bob Regnerus's rec-ommended video tool at **TheLeadsKing VideoService.com**.

You can point to the area on the computer screen where the opt-in form will appear and say, "Type your name and e-mail address in this box."

Audio. Now that internet video is easy to record and distribute, there's not much need for audio content, especially on a landing page. If you have the ability to add an audio introduction to your landing page, you're better off spending the same amount of time putting up a video introduction instead.

To easily incorporate audio into your website, use our recommended audio tool at **TheLeadsKingAudioService.com**.

However, downloadable audio is a good thing to offer your prospects in certain situations, so there may still be a need for audio content on your landing page.

Flash animation. Animation has its place on some information marketing websites, but that place is usually in a sales presentation rather than on a landing page. Unless you absolutely need it, stay away from Flash elements or anything else that might distract your visitors.

Your Design

We tell our clients not to get preoccupied with website design. Sophisticated color palettes, Flash animation and Java applications can make a website more impressive, but they rarely make it more effective. We've seen plenty of businesses succeed with good products and bad-looking websites, but we've never seen a great-looking website save a business with a bad product.

You want your visitors to pay attention to your offer and call to action, not your sense of color. Use a design that's effective without being noticeable. Put some thought into the placement of your landing page's key elements, and use colors and typefaces that are easy on the eyes.

When it comes to landing page design, the most important thing is to know what's going above the fold. "Above the fold" is an old newspaper term for the stories that appear on the top of the front page—the ones you see when you look at a folded paper in a stack or in a box. It also refers to the top section of a web page—the part you see before you scroll down.

The key elements of your landing page should be above the fold. This includes your headline, your video (if you use one), your offer and your call to action. It's easy to scroll down a web page, but many

For more free landing page examples and ideas for your business, visit **InternetInfoMarketing Book.com/landingpages**.

visitors won't bother to do it, so you need to put the important stuff right in front of them.

Optimizing Your Landing Page for Google

A significant percentage (maybe over 50 percent) of the traffic to your landing page will come from Google. Google handles roughly half of the world's search engine traffic, and Google AdWords is the world's largest pay-per-click ad service. Keep this in mind when you design your landing page.

Google wants to provide high-quality information to its users, so it evaluates each page it includes in its organic search results and in its paid advertising. Each page is assigned a "quality score," which is based on elements on the page as well as the response the page gets from Google's users. The higher your quality score, the more people Google will send your way and the less your traffic will cost you.

We take an in-depth look at getting more traffic from Google in Chapter 8. Right now, let's look at the things Google wants to see on your landing page.

Good Content

Google looks for "relevance and originality" in your content. Relevant content is closely connected with the search term that brought a visitor to your site. Original content is content that is unique to your website, so write your own copy rather than recycling text you found on other sites.

Transparency

What we call "credibility," Google calls "transparency." Google looks for guarantees, company contact information and privacy policies on landing pages, and it rewards the pages that provide them. Google also looks for misleading language and advertisements disguised as content, so make sure your copy is clear and accurate.

Google likes landing pages that provide content to visitors without requiring them to register. This is a bit of a problem because the point of your landing page is to collect your visitors' contact information right away. If you provide a few links to pages with relevant content (maybe on your brochure-style site, if you have one), you should be able to avoid problems in this area. Just make sure those links don't get in the way of the more important items: your copy, offer and call to action.

Navigability

Google expects your landing page to make it easy for visitors to find what they're looking for. Complicated navigation, lots of pop-up ads and slow load times will hurt your quality score, but if you've followed the guidelines in this chapter, you won't have those problems.

Landing Page Examples

The two examples below—from **DentistryForDiabetics.com** and the Executive Education Program at Dartmouth's Tuck School of

Business—illustrate what effective landing pages should look like.

Dentistry for Diabetics. The Dentistry for Diabetics landing page is a perfect example. At the top is a bold, compelling headline aimed right at the program's target audience. Directly below the headline are the other critical "above the fold" elements: the offer, the call to action and the opt-in form.

FIGURE 4-1. Screenshot 1 of a landing page for Dentistry for Diabetics

A short (under three minutes) video from Dr. Charles Martin welcomes the visitor, introduces the Dentistry for Diabetics program and asks the visitor to opt in by completing the form on the right side of

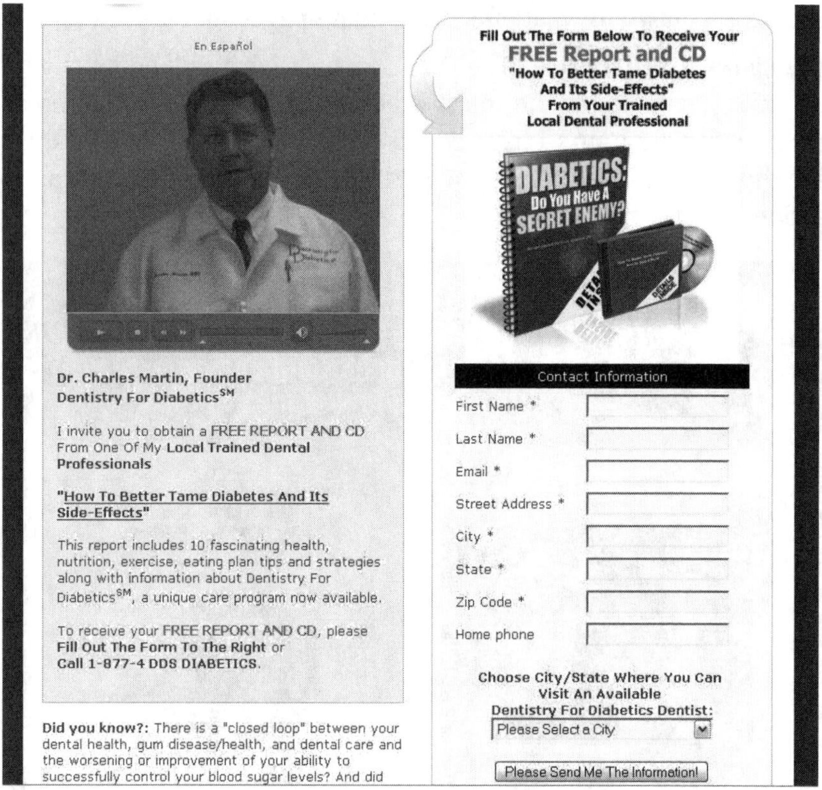

FIGURE 4-2. Screenshot 2 of a landing page for Dentistry for Diabetics

the screen. Nothing on this page is trying to sell the actual Dentistry for Diabetics program—the only call to action has to do with the free offer and opt-in form.

Further down the page, the visitor is presented with additional details about the free offer, a patient testimonial and another version of the call to action.

Tuck Executive Education at Dartmouth. The landing page for Dartmouth's Executive Education program has the same key elements: a large, benefit-driven headline, a prominent opt-in page and a clear call to action. The offer and call to action are made in text rather than video, but it's still easy to understand what the page is asking of the visitor—note the use of highlighting and the arrow beneath the call to action.

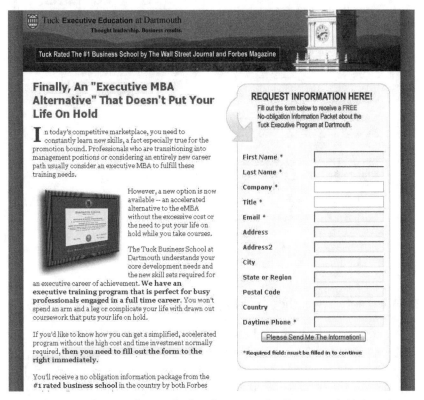

FIGURE 4-3. Screen shot 1 of a landing page for Dartmouth University

This page makes use of powerful images, such as the Dartmouth clock tower and a sample diploma, to establish the credibility of the program and the benefits being offered.

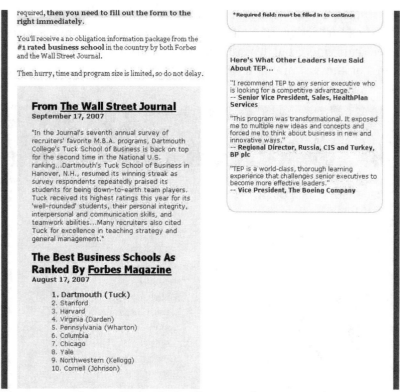

FIGURE 4-4. Screenshot 2 of a landing page for Dartmouth University

Take a close look at the button under the opt-in form. It doesn't say "Submit" or "Enter," but rather repeats the call to action as a request from the visitor: "Please Send Me the Information!" Little enhancements like that can do a lot to increase the desirability of your landing page offer.

Getting the Most Out of Your Landing Page

Don't walk away once your landing page is up and running. The most successful internet information marketing businesses are those that constantly refine and improve their marketing campaigns. To get the most out of your website, you need to use the information you collect on your landing page, and you need to find ways to improve your page's performance.

Building and Using Your List

The list of e-mail or street addresses you build on your landing page is one of your business's most valuable assets. Everyone on that list came to your website because they saw an advertisement or a link that caught their interest. When they got to your site, they were interested enough in what they saw on your landing page to submit their information to you. Those are the people you want to sell to, now and in the future.

The first use of your list is following up with people who opted in on your landing page, but didn't make a purchase after their first visit. We talk about your follow-up campaign in Chapter 7.

Of course, follow-up isn't the only thing your list is good for. You can jumpstart marketing campaigns for other products and services by sending promotional e-mails to the people on your list, and you can get ideas for new products and services by soliciting feedback or questions from the people on your list.

Send e-mails once a week or as often as once a day when you're in the early stages of your follow-up campaign. Whatever the schedule, be sure your e-mails are timely and relevant, or you'll notice a lot of people using the "unsubscribe" feature of your mailing list.

Your landing page is the best tool for building your list, but you can add to it from other sources. Solicit the contact information of your existing customers (in return for a discount, perhaps) and ask the people who read your articles and blogs to sign up for a monthly newsletter, even if they're not shopping for anything at the moment.

Protecting your list is just as important as building your list. If you value your customers, don't sell their contact information. You'll keep your existing customers and find new ones more easily if you have a reputation for honoring your privacy policy.

Tracking Your Results

An internet information marketing campaign involves lots of trial-and-error testing. Every time you start a campaign, you need to try out different pricing strategies, different offers, different headlines and different copy to see what generates the most interest from your visitors. When you pay close attention to your statistics, you'll know right away whether your changes are helping or hurting your campaign. You (or someone who works for you) should be looking at day-by-day changes in your traffic and opt-in rate, especially at the beginning of a campaign.

It's best to make one change at a time. If you add a horrible new headline to your landing page on the same day that you replace a bad offer with a good one, your opt-in rate might not change, and you'll learn nothing. If you make those changes one week apart, you'll quickly know that you need to keep the new offer and go back to the drawing board for a new headline. The more traffic your site receives, the less time you need to allow for your changes to show their effect.

We talk more about tracking your website performance in Chapters 8 and 9.

Keeping an Eye on the Competition

Study and identify what other information marketers are doing on their websites. If you want your visitors to stop when they get to your landing page, you need to know what they've already seen.

When you're just getting started, spend a few days looking at the sites of the other businesses in your market. Start by doing some basic searches and looking at the sites that appear at the top of the paid results and the organic results. Those are the businesses that are doing the best job, so they'll have a few things to teach you. If you don't have the time, hire someone to surf the web for you and make notes.

You'll also want to opt in on the landing pages of at least a few of your competitors. You'll get a closer look at their sales materials, and you'll see what they're doing with their e-mail lists. You may even want to buy some of their products if you're in a highly competitive market—the more you know about your competition, the better.

Even when you've established yourself as the "go-to" authority, and your products and services are selling, you should always know what your competitors are up to. After all, it's a sure thing that they're watching you.

"Coaching Millions" Is Music to Milana Leshinsky's Ears

Info-Marketer Profile

This is the story of a music teacher from the Ukraine who immigrated to the United States, took up web design and ended up creating a successful coaching business.

Milana Leshinsky's story goes all the way back to her childhood half a world away. "I have studied music my whole life, since the age of eight," she says, "and I always knew I would be a music teacher." That goal changed for Milana when she moved to the United States, where she lost interest in teaching. "The music education system is much different here," she explains. "In Russia, if you study something, you do it to become an athlete, a dancer or a musician. You don't do it because your mom wants you to get some extracurricular activities. It's a different attitude in general, and I just lost my passion to teach music."

After having her first child, Milana decided to change careers. She went into business administration and later computer programming. Her creative bent led her to do web design for an insurance company and a newspaper. Later, she began working freelance. Over time, Milana noticed that certain types of clients kept hiring her to design websites. They were coaches, and at that time, she had no idea what a coach was. "I was clueless," Milana smiles, "but after the third time a coach came to me for a website, I took notice!"

Milana started investigating what coaching is, who coaches ➤

are and what was going on in the coaching industry. After 1½ years of research, she was ready to open the Association of Coaching & Consulting Professionals on the Web (ACC POW), and she started a membership site for coaches, using all the materials she had gathered during her research.

Hold on. Milana went from not even knowing what a coach was to creating an association for coaches? How did that happen? "If I had to go back and put my finger on the moment when all of a sudden I became known in coaching, I would have to attribute it to two factors," she says. "First, one of the clients who hired me to do website design was a coach and part of a coaching team. She invited me to be a coach on her team. I didn't consider myself a coach, but I said OK anyway. Later on, I wrote an e-book, *How to Grow Your Coaching Practice on the Internet*, and she wrote the foreword for it. Because she was established in the coaching world, her partnership in my e-book gave me a lot of credibility. The second thing that propelled my success and let me niche in the coaching industry was a website called **Tele-Class.com** by Thomas Leonard. Advertising on this site where coaches gathered was my doorway into the industry."

Milana populated her website by using monthly tele-seminars with invited guests. At first, success came slowly. "My first tele-class, I had one person come," she laughs. Her next one was more successful, with 30 people on the line, but she still had a little something to learn. "I started to get the fact that if I just did a tele-seminar, nothing was going to happen," Milana explains, "so, at the end of the tele-class, I offered a program that I did not have yet. I had a concept of the program, and I thought if anybody was interested, I could quickly design it since I had all of the content in my head. I had seven people registered for the tele-seminar, so I called my yet-to-be-created product '7 Habits of Most Successful Coaches.'"

➡️

The offer worked, and suddenly, Milana had coaches enrolling in her program and joining her membership site. "The offer was a 12-week program based on the tele-class," she explains. "It taught how to make a website that would allow you to enroll clients directly from the site. It was everything I had learned by working with coaches designing their websites. Basically, I had compared the websites of coaches who were broke to the websites of coaches who were doing really well. I noticed that successful coaches have products, names for themselves, processes and follow-up sequences. Their sites look extremely professional. So, I gathered all of these factors into a program, and I coached people who came to me and said, 'Milana, I have this coaching website. I invested thousands of dollars into it, but it doesn't seem to bring any business.' Then, I would critique the site and work with the client to create content to rework it."

It took some trial and error to hit on what Milana's customers would pay for her membership site. "I tried different pricing models," she says. "I started with $97 a year, but that didn't work very well. I had only about 10 members, so I switched to $39.95 per quarter. That worked, and I still use that pricing today." Actually, Milana lets her site run "in the background" now. "I have not done any updates for at least a year," she says. "With everything else going on in my business, it has remained a part of my offering, but it's no longer part of my product funnel. But it's a great back-up income, and I don't do anything to market it."

Another thing Milana doesn't do anymore is website design. "I had lost interest, and I couldn't get clients," she recalls. "I remember walking with my husband in the park and talking about this, and he said, 'Why don't you just lower the pricing.' So, I did. I went down to $250 for a six-page website—and I attracted the jerkiest clients I ever had in my life! I hated that particular period of my business life, so I just stopped marketing for these clients."

Milana needed a breakthrough to get to the next level of her business. She found what she needed during a mastermind session, "Infopreneur's Think Tank," with Sterling Valentine. "I wanted to do a conference," Milana says, "but I didn't like to go to live conferences myself. I was a mom with two children, so I was looking for a way to do a conference without actually doing a live conference. I thought I could do something similar to Sterling's mastermind group for coaches over the telephone. Then, a friend of mine suggested opening it up to the public. I did that and gave my program a different name: tele-summit. With Sterling, I created a worldwide global event for coaches that lasted for three years."

Milana went on to teach others how to do tele-summits for their industries. "Before I did the tele-summit, the word simply didn't exist. Now, if you do a web search on the word tele-summit, you'll see thousands of results," she says. "The idea caught on, and that was my big break."

Tele-Summit

A tele-summit is a telephone-based, multiday event. A tele-summit is a unique opportunity because people can participate for several days in training programs, but not have to spend all the time and money to travel. The benefit for the promoter is not having to book hotels and taking on all the financial risks associated with a live event.

Milana's tele-summits appealed to people who didn't want to travel, and she attracted people from all over the world. "On the first call of my tele-summit, there were participants from 17 different

➤

countries!" she exclaims. "By doing a conference virtually, I was able to tap into a segment of the coaching industry that other organizations weren't reaching with their live events."

Her first tele-summit ran for eight days, and the $60,000 she netted from registration fees and sales online doubled her annual income of $30,000. "That was huge for me," Milana says, "but obviously, the chain reaction happened afterwards. Now I'm known as the gal who did the tele-summit," she laughs.

By hosting a tele-summit featuring 12 experts in the coaching industry, Milana was able to go from being relatively unknown to being right in the center of the industry. This new industry awareness of who she was increased her revenue from all her other products, plus it allowed her to book experts for her second tele-summit more easily. "I was overwhelmed with people trying to get in as a speaker for my second event."

Always looking to improve her business, Milana sought the advice of a coach when she realized she had too many products with no streamlined process to move a client from one product to the next. "I was so much into product development that I ended up with about 27 different mini-products, 27 different mini-sites selling a product on CD or as a digital file. With so many products, it was hard to market. My business felt very fragmented, so my coach suggested folding all of my products into one to create a system."

Milana took that advice and created a home study course called *Coaching Millions*, based on her book *Coaching Millions Business Building System*. The course is for coaches who want to build their businesses as well as for info-preneurs who want to go beyond selling info-products.

The other part of Milana's business is her "Coaching Business Mastery" program. She says it's a "very cleverly disguised home business course, plus an implementation program." The core of the mastery program is Milana's home study course. "The only difference is I'm also offering an implementation program," she explains.

People who enroll in the "Coaching Business Mastery" program receive Milana's home study course, and two weeks later begin the implementation program. They get on a group mentoring call every Monday. They ask questions based on what they've heard or read in the home study course. "So, instead of my trying to teach the material over and over again, they actually have the materials. It's inside the home study course," Milana says.

An important piece of the program is accountability. "I hate doing accountability because it's like dragging somebody by their hair and saying, 'Did you do it? Did you do it?' But if they don't do it, they aren't going to succeed with my program, and then they're going to come back to me and ask for a refund. So, for me, it was very important to create accountability without having to drag the person by their hair to complete the task."

Milana developed a feature called "Post Your Documents" to create accountability without "hair dragging." Every week, her clients are asked automatically through her autoresponder to post a document they've developed for that week. "Whether it's a freebie, a special report, niche market research results, a follow-up sequence they're developing or a joint venture proposal that they're working on, I want to see their documents," she says. "Whether I give them feedback or not is irrelevant. The point is that they are reminded every week to post their documents so I can see they're sticking with the program."

A great side benefit to Milana's accountability feature is that she's building an inventory of real-life examples with before and after results.

Chapter 5

King Presentation

Converting Visitors Into Customers

A FTER KING SALUTATION HAS WELCOMED VISITORS TO THE KING-dom and convinced them to take the next steps on their journeys, it's time for King Presentation to take over.

King Presentation specializes in ideas. He knows why visitors have come to the kingdom, and he knows how to convince them that he has the answers to their questions. He inspires his visitors to act, whether they're hesitant or highly motivated.

When your sales prospects opt in on your landing page, they become your sales leads. They've announced that they're interested in learning more about your product or service and that they trust you enough to enter into a relationship with you.

The next step in that relationship is the sales process. In this chapter, you learn how to use your sales presentation to turn your leads into customers.

After the Opt-In

Let's start by talking about what happens after visitors opt in on your landing page. You can't just leave them on the page after they hit the "Submit" button, so what's the next step? The ultimate goal, of course, is to make your sales presentation. Before you get to that, you need to wrap up the conversation you started on your landing page by thanking visitors for opting in and telling them what's going to happen next. To do that, you have two options:

A Confirmation Page

This provides information about the delivery of your landing page offer. If you deliver the offer via e-mail, the page should tell the visitor to check his or her e-mail after allowing time for the e-mail to be sent (the sooner that happens, the better).

If the offer involves participation in a tele-seminar or a live conference, the confirmation page should provide the event details, such as date, time and place, or call-in number. If those details are not yet determined, tell the visitor when to expect a full confirmation by e-mail or regular mail.

If sales leads get access to a membership site for opting in, your confirmation page should provide their login ID and password. If you need time to generate those, tell the visitor to look for an e-mail.

If the offer is being sent by mail or delivery service, the page should repeat the details of the offer and provide an estimated delivery date. If you use a shipping method that allows for tracking, tell the visitor to look for an e-mail with a tracking number after the shipment goes out.

A Download Page

If your offer is something in electronic form, like an e-book, an audio file or a video file, you can let visitors download it themselves rather than receive it in an e-mail.

This is definitely the way to go if your offer is a large file, which most e-books and multimedia files are. Downloads can be a little tricky, so you may want to use an outside service to host your download page.

What Happens Next?

After your visitors conclude their conversations with King Salutation, it's time to introduce them to King Presentation. You may have mentioned your products or services on your landing page, but if you did things right, you didn't try to sell them. Now that you have your leads' contact information and you're sure that they're interested, you can make your sales pitch.

How you make your sales presentation should be determined by the product or service you're selling and how you plan to close your sales. There are three types of sales presentations you can use in your internet information marketing campaign:

- **The online sales presentation:** A web page or series of web pages that gives a complete sales presentation to your leads.

- **The tele-seminar:** A sales presentation delivered over the phone or in an audio recording.

- **The "Shock-and-Awe" package:** A box of sales materials, including CDs, DVDs, books, letters and samples, delivered to the sales lead's home.

Each of these sales models has strengths and weaknesses, depending on the product or service it's used to sell. They all depend on the same thing to get them started, though: a visitor opting in on your landing page. Before we get into the differences between these sales presentation models, let's look at what else they have in common.

Five Goals for Every Sales Presentation

The internet gives you more options for presenting your sales materials, but it doesn't change the basic rules of consumer behavior. Whether you do your selling online, over the phone or through the mail, you need to show that you understand what your leads are thinking and what will motivate them to make a purchase.

In his book *The Ultimate Marketing Plan*, Dan Kennedy lists five things that every sales presentation must accomplish. We look at these five tasks using a classic example: selling water.

Let's say you're selling water-treatment systems. That's never an easy sell because there's a free alternative—water from the tap—available at all times. If you want to stay in business, you have to convince your customers that they can't get by without your treatment system. Here's how you do it:

Five Tasks for Every Sales Presentation

Sales presentation task #1: Describe the problem. The first job of your sales presentation is to describe the problem your product or service solves and to convince your customers they have that problem.

In our water-filtration example, the first thing you have to do is convince your customers that tap water is not acceptable. You would most likely start by listing the substances lurking in tap water, such as chemicals, bacteria and traces of drugs. Fear is a great motivator, so you want to make your leads think about what those foreign substances are doing to them every time they drink tap water.

If you have access to specific information about the water supply in your customers' location, you would use it to convince them they're ingesting those dangerous substances every day.

Sales presentation task #2: Describe the solution. Once you've convinced your sales leads they have a problem, you need to position your type of product or service as the only viable solution to the problem.

Keep in mind that the *type* of solution is what's important at this stage. You're not selling your particular brand yet.

The goal here is to eliminate other solutions from consideration in your customers' minds, and that requires more than simply describing the benefits of water-treatment systems. You have to name the other possibilities and explain why they're not good solutions. To sell the idea of water-treatment systems, you could point out that bottled water is more expensive than home-treated water and that it's often taken from municipal water sources without additional filtration. You could also describe the futility of complaining to the city or county government about the problem.

In certain situations, you won't need to spend much time on tasks #1 and #2. If you were selling dog food rather than water-treatment systems, you wouldn't have to convince your customers they had a hungry dog or the solution to that problem was to buy dog food.

Don't skip over those first points entirely, though. When you're talking about a universal or obvious problem, you have a good opportunity to make a personal connection by using a personal story or a little bit of humor.

Sales presentation task #3: Separate your solution from the competition's. Now, in step 3, you separate your brand of water-treatment systems from all the others on the market. Whatever sets you apart from your competitors—proprietary technology, innovative design, government endorsements—this is the time to play it up.

Naming the competing brands is usually not the best idea. You might mention competitors your leads weren't familiar with, causing them to shop around a little more (you can also run into legal trouble if you're not careful). If there's one big name in the water-treatment marketplace, you can talk about the "leading brand" or "the big guys" and feel confident your audience knows which company you're talking about.

Sales presentation task #4: Justify your price. The next step is to justify the price of your water-treatment system. Break the price down into a certain amount of pennies or dollars per day, or compare it to the cost of buying bottled water every day. If price is a barrier in your sales process, you should anticipate the objections your customers are likely to have.

Sales presentation task #5: Inspire immediate action. Finally, you want to convince your customers to take action right away. You could do this by referring to the health concerns you mentioned early in the letter: Every day that your customers drink normal tap water is another day they're consuming those contaminants. You can also provide special offers or discounts and tie them to a response deadline.

Three Profit-Proven Models for Sales Presentations

No matter how you present your sales materials, always start with that same five-point outline. It's simply the most effective way to make a sale. The most successful information marketers accomplish those five tasks in every sales presentation. With that in mind, let's take a closer look at our three profit-proven models for sales presentations.

To further understand how to turn words into sales, visit **InternetInfoMarketing Book.com/copywriting**.

Model #1: The Online Sales Presentation

An online sales presentation is any sales presentation delivered over the internet. It might be a simple electronic sales letter, or it might be a sophisticated multimedia presentation that incorporates video demonstrations, slideshows and interactive web pages.

Online sales letters. An online sales letter is usually a single web page. In many ways, an online sales letter is similar to a landing page. A good online sales letter has a clear, compelling headline, an appealing offer and a call to action. It asks for a specific action and provides specific instructions. In this case, your offer is your actual product or service rather than a small item to get a prospect's attention, and rather than asking for contact information, your sales letter's call to action is a request for a sale.

Even though the content is somewhat different, all the same rules for landing pages apply to a sales letter. In most cases, you should only try to sell one item or product line with a single sales letter. If you offer many products and services, you should have separate sales letters (and probably separate landing pages) for each.

In all cases, your online sales letter copy should be well written and direct. Include testimonials and other sources of credibility, and make the page free of unnecessary links and text.

Once again, the simpler you can make things, the easier it is for people to buy from you. Make sure your potential customers understand what you're selling, what it costs and how they can buy it.

When you write your copy and design your page, remember that some of your sales leads may be shopping online for the first time. Those people may need extra help, but their money is just as good as anyone else's.

Multimedia presentations. In the past few years, it's become easier to incorporate audio, video and animation in websites. When used correctly, these elements make online sales presentations more engaging and compelling.

Multimedia sales presentations take many forms. You can record a video version of a live sales presentation in which you or someone else addresses the sales lead directly. You can record a PowerPoint slideshow and play it with voice-over commentary. If you have the resources, you can use Adobe Flash or QuickTime to create more sophisticated, interactive presentations that combine slideshows, video and animation.

As you'd expect, multimedia presentations are more expensive and time-consuming to produce than simple online sales letters, but if you're selling more expensive products or services, the additional cost will probably pay off.

Using your landing page offer as an online sales presentation. In certain circumstances, your landing page offer can serve as your sales presentation.

This is easy to do when you're selling with tele-seminars and Shock-and-Awe packages, as you'll see here. When you're using online sales presentations, it's a little more difficult. Your landing page visitors might be interested in an offer to take part in a tele-seminar, but they won't see as much appeal in an offer to look at a sales letter or a slideshow.

If you plan to use your landing page offer as your sales presentation, make sure it includes information your sales prospects will want to see. Video demonstrations are the most effective way to combine landing page offers and sales materials, but reports, e-books and white papers can also do the job.

To return to our water-treatment example, your combination landing page offer/sales presentation might be a free report on the contaminants in your prospects' drinking water. A detailed report would do a great job of achieving a sales presentation's first goal: describing the problem. After you've done that, you can move seamlessly into the rest of your sales presentation. If you did a good job with the first step, your sales lead won't notice the report has turned into a sales presentation.

When to use an online sales presentation. Online sales presentations work best when you're asking your leads to make a purchase online. This means, in most cases, that you're selling products or services with short buying cycles that aren't expensive. E-books, newsletter subscriptions and membership site registrations are examples of information products you might expect to sell online.

Bigger-ticket items, such as seminar registrations and DVD collections, can go either way. You might be able to sell them online, or you might be better off collecting sales leads and following up by phone or mail. It depends on your market, your products and your prices.

If you're not sure what you should do, try selling online and offline at the same time and tracking your results. If your online sales presentation works as well as your offline materials, you can save money and time by sending more leads to your website. If online sales don't work, start using your website for lead generation.

If your products or services are very expensive or highly personal—coaching or consulting services, for example—you won't have much luck closing sales on your website. Focus your online efforts on generating leads, and use either tele-seminars or the Shock-and-Awe package to do your selling.

Delivering your online sales presentation. The simplest delivery method for an online sales presentation is to provide a link to the presentation from your confirmation page or download page (whichever follows your landing page).

You can actually present this as though you're doing your sales lead a favor. Thank him or her for opting in, provide the relevant details about your offer and then say something along the lines of "While you're here, we'd be doing you a disservice if we didn't mention that we have a fantastic new product. Click *HERE* to find out more!"

If your landing page offer is doing double duty as a sales presentation, you don't have to worry about this step. After your confirmation page or download page, you can either send your sales lead to your homepage or to another page with information that supports the sales presentation.

Sample Online Sales Presentations

Let's look at two examples of effective online sales presentations. One is a simple online sales presentation, and the other incorporates some multimedia elements. The first is Matthew Gillogly's website, **BeMatts Apprentice.com**, contains a great example of an online sales letter.

How would you like to have me, Matthew Gillogly personally Mentor you on your real estate investing business? To show you Exactly how to set up a real estate investing business that Brings sellers and buyers together, without me having To be involved.

If YOU Answered YES – You Must Devour Every Word Of This Letter Because....

Investor, If You Qualify – I Will Personally Work With You Side-By-Side To Build A Sizzling Real Estate Money Machine

(CAUTION: ONLY 4 PEOPLE WILL BE SELECTED)

If you're serious about multiplying your income, and gaining personal life that you control, you're invited to apply to be my "Apprentice" for 12 months. But you must act now....

Dear Fellow Real Estate Investor,

How would you like to have a real live real estate investing guru work personally with you in your business for 12 full months? Showing you how to capitalize on the deals in this troubled real estate market.

No, this is not a joke.

There is no bait and switch.

I have not lost my mind.

The truth is... for 4 very lucky individuals I will work side by side with them in their real estate business. I've never done this before and I don't know when, if ever, I'll do it again. So read this letter very carefully, because what I'm about to share with you will unquestionably change the lives for 4 investors nationwide.

But first I must ask you 5 questions. **What would it be worth to you to have me personally...**

FIGURE 5-1. Example of an online, long-form sales letter

1. Mentor you in your real estate investing business? To get on the phone with you 2 times a month, review and structure deals?
2. **Have me set up your marketing campaigns, newspaper ads, order your telephone pole signs, set up your answering service and website.** Basically do everything but hang up the signs in your hometown to get the phone ringing with motivated sellers or buyers.
3. **Fly into your hometown and spend one full 24 hour period where we call sellers, buyers, talk with realtors and structure deals,** so that by the time I get back on the plane you have deals in hand.
4. Take you under my personal wing and show you EXACTLY what you must do to make it in a Troubled Real Estate Market.
5. **Bring in my secret list of 'loss mitigators' to negotiate your short sales,** taking a huge load off your shoulders?

What would you pay for something like this?

I asked my brother Dan who's been investing longer than I've been investing and he said he'd pay in excess of $30,000.00

When I told my wife, Sarah, she just about jumped out of the chair. *"Honey, that'd be incredible. My gosh! People would love to see you in action, looking over your shoulder while you do the deal! Plus you're going to generate leads for them! Wow, when we were starting out we would have killed for a program like that!"*

I then thought I'd go to some folks who are not related to me to get their opinion. Matt & Kim Vestrand, long time Platinum members thought that'd be a better deal than the Platinum program. *"It would completely changed the way we did business and leap frogged us to the top of the hill in investing."*

I brainstormed this with a group of my hand picked real estate coaches in Charlotte a few weeks ago. Of the 7 in the room, **5 pulled me aside and wanted in IF I offered the program....** And these are experienced investors.

Before I Tell You All About The Apprentice Program, Answer These Questions....

What's really going on in your business? Are you staying ahead of the competition? Are you getting your fair share of great deals? Are you working too hard and not getting the results you want? Do you long for a coach, a mentor you can contact 24/7/365 to get the answers you need?

If everything is perfect and you're totally happy with the status quo, then THROW THIS LETTER AWAY... YOU DON'T NEED ME!

But if you'd like to improve your business's profitability, close more deals in less time and start cashing checks like those other investors you read about, then keep reading!

The big question you have to ask yourself is...

Am I living the lifestyle that I envisioned when I started investing in real estate. Are you able to implement all the great ideas you've learned in real estate?

A little over 7 years ago, I started investing in real estate. I was introduced to it at a seminar. I immediately started implementing things and started on a quest for new ideas and information that has never stopped. In fact, every year, I invest more and more money on my education through books, tapes, CD's, seminars and mastermind groups. And each and every year, **it is by far the biggest payoff investment I make.** To continue to be successful I need to continually sharpen my skills and associate myself with other like-minded people. I have several mentors who have helped me along my journey.

FIGURE 5-1. Example of an online, long-form sales letter (continued)

My discovery is not unusual. I've never seen a superstar in any profession who wasn't' relentlessly molded by a mentor for most of their career. For example...

Michael Jordan was "cut" by his high school basketball team before his coach stepped forward and personally mentored him to become the greatest basketball player of all time. **Tiger Woods** is the youngest four time winner of the Masters and one of the greatest players of all time. Even with all of his skill and talent, he credits his success to his coach, in fact, many coaches. He still uses a coach today.

No one has ever won an Olympic Gold medal without a coach. Actors and actresses like: Matt Damon, Jennifer Garner and Jim Carey all have coaches. And according to Forbes magazine, more and more of the nation's top entrepreneurs, business owners and CEO's are all using coaches to help achieve a new level of success.

Regardless Of The Skills And Talents You Bring To Any Profession, Achieving Success All Alone Is A Grinding, Almost Hopeless Uphill Battle

If you've ever felt overwhelmed or stressed-out or felt like throwing it all into the trash, because it seemed like an impossible task to build a business that supports your ideal lifestyle, then you'll want to read every word I'm about to tell you.

For the past five years, I've personally coached over 2,414 investors nationwide. Over 309 of those students, were one on one coaching students, where I got on the phone with them each and every month to pour over their businesses, identify log jams and help lift their businesses to new heights.

Since the beginning of 2007, I've taken some time off from the one on one coaching world. Frankly, I needed a break. There have been a few students here and there I've taken on to mentor, but for the most part, I've laid low.

Why you ask? Was I burned out? Were the students no longer successful? Nope, it came down to this... With a changing market for investing, **I needed to take some time off and develop new strategies and coaching techniques to make my students even more successful.**

I didn't want to keep offering the same old strategies and techniques. After all, real estate has changed and to have the right way to invest in this down market is critical to building long-term wealth and quick cash.

So I went back to the drawing board to create a truly one on one "apprentice" environment. One where you can have direct exclusive access to me, get your questions answered, network and mastermind with other like minded investors, make serious money in real estate and do it all based on Biblical Principles.

Here's what I've added to the Apprentice Program put together and TESTED with other investors to ensure it's the absolute best one on one coaching program for real estate investors in America. Here is what we do in a typical month.

- **Personal Coaching Calls:** Each and every month, I get together one on one and personally with each of my Elite members where we discuss what's going on in their business.

  These calls happen once a month where you get 20 minutes with me, your personal coach. You drive the content of those calls. We discuss what's gone well since the last call, what you are struggling with and where you need to focus for the next two weeks. *Just like a top pro athlete's "coach", I'll stay on your back and hold you accountable.*

  I'll keep you on track every month so it's darned near impossible to NOT reach your goals.

FIGURE 5-1. Example of an online, long-form sales letter (continued)

- **"Ask The Expert": Have a burning question involving your real estate business?** You can simply ask myself or my staff any question involving your real estate business right on-line. Need timely help with the paperwork? Marketing questions? Need assistance with negotiation? Not even sure what to do next? Just "Ask The Expert" and you will have a response to your issue within one business day!
- **"What would Matt Gillogly do" Deal Reviews for buying and selling: Have a buyer or seller lead and not sure what to do?** Not sure what to offer to pay for a property? Or, even more critical – what to accept from prospective buyers? Remember: your tenant-buyers are holding your property hostage until they purchase it! Make sure you get them in and get them in right... or you'll be sorry!
- Monthly **"Virtual" Online Video Training.** You'll get a brand new video and telecoaching call where I'll share my specific insights on biblically based real estate investing strategies. There's a fresh, new topic each and every month for you to watch via video online. Each training module, no more than 30 minutes in length, delivers exacting "How To" information for each topic. For instance:

  - **How to sell houses fast in a troubled market**
  - How to recognize each of the 4 personality types and what weapons you should use against them to create a win/win in every negotiation
  - **How to buy properties in a down trending market (and what particular properties you should avoid at all costs)**
  - How to research your market, target the best buy and sell opportunities, and create an unstoppable momentum in your business
  - **Using influence ethically to close more profitable deals**
  - Secrets of accountable advertising: How to set up your automated systems to find and qualify sellers, buyers, and tenants without ever picking up the phone
  - **Quick cash infusions: What deals to set up to quickly fill your pockets with cash**

  After you've had the opportunity to watch the training video, I'll host a live 90 minute, open-line teleconference to answer any questions on the topic or any deals you may have pending.
- **98.7% Automation of your buying and selling houses business: I'll show you how you can totally automate your business (well almost).** After all... somebody has to give the deal approvals an ok, and deposit the checks, which I strongly believe should be you. But that's it.

  Everything else – from marketing towards buyers and sellers, to pre screening and pre-qualifying your buyers and sellers, must be automated. The purpose of this business is to free your time up – not consume you.

  If you're going bonkers manning the phone lines or managing web sites or spending more than a few minutes on the phone each day you aren't using systems to their full potential. It is very likely you are standing in the way of your own success - stumbling over pebbles instead of climbing mountains.

- Downloadable forms and paperwork: **All the paperwork you need to buy and sell properties will be right here for download.** Don't even dare use some generic forms – the forms I give you have been up and down the court systems in all 50 states.
- Monthly audio interview and download: **Each month I interview an expert in business. From renegade Christians to successful real estate investors to marketing wizards.** Each and every month you'll be able to download the audio interview to your CD player or iPod to listen to at your leisure. Be sure to take notes... because each expert I interview is freely giving out information that will be worth thousands of dollars to your business.
- The Renegade Christian Online Forum: **Discuss current hot topics with other Renegade Christians.** Anything from market trends, successes and trials, etc.... This forum is the central location and hang out for the who's who of successful Christian real estate investors and entrepenuers.
- Follow "The Big Deals" with Matt: **Think of this as a true "Reality Show" with myself and one of my students.** As students get deals into the pipeline, we'll give you blow by blow updates. Think of this as looking over my shoulder as other investors are coached along to success. Plus any of my personal big deals will be highlighted and there for your viewing.

FIGURE 5-1. Example of an online, long-form sales letter (continued)

- **Checklists for every step of every system in your business. Your site includes checklists for buying properties by taking over the sellers mortgage, controlling with an 'option to buy', straight cash and traditional purchases.** Every type of transaction is covered with a specific checklist. In fact, if you can think of a checklist that isn't there... it is probably something you shouldn't be doing!
- **Downloadable Marketing pieces for you to customize. We provide you the marketing pieces** in Microsoft Publisher, PDF, and Microsoft Word (when possible) so that you can customize and tailor the piece with your name and numbers quickly and easily. No matter what computer program or platform you use, you'll be able to edit the document the way you need it.
- **Marketing case studies: Do you ever wonder how well the marketing materials 'gurus' sell really work?** Do you ever look at a marketing piece and want to throw up... and wonder "Why on earth does that work?" Well... here is a first nowhere ever done before. All marketing pieces we provide will also be a report of who it was sent to, how it was used, why, and how well it worked. These are real world pieces used, sent to real buyers and real sellers.

Think of all of these bonuses and benefits as weapons in your arsenal. New battles require new strategies but with the help of God and the basic equipment that I'm providing you here will ensure you overcome.

I'm Not Done Yet.....

Once you join my Apprentice Program, you not only receive all of the bonuses listed above, but you'll also receive complimentary attendance at my upcoming...

And There's One More Thing I'll Give You When You Act Now!

I'll host not one, but TWO full days of Masterminding where we'll go into each persons business. You'll receive specialized mentoring in a small group environment. *Imagine getting away from your business with other like minded investors and sharing as a group.*

Plus, you'll get to attend a total of three (3) of these Masterminds throughout the year. Receiving specialized training from me in a very small boardroom style setting.

We will discuss new strategies and detail them A-Z so the guesswork is virtually eliminated on how, when and where to apply them.

I'm Not Done Yet(Part II)...

Plus as an Apprentice, you'll receive exclusive access to my Mr. X. Who is Mr. X and why is this important to you?

Well with the real estate markets correcting, **now is one of the best times to buy pre-foreclosure property. Banks are taking back property at record numbers.** Why just last week, two mortgage hedge funds closed!

As you may or may not know, my background is in pre-foreclosures. I've been involved in over 150 short sales. I love the money from the pre-foreclosure business, but HATE doing the short sale. My Mr. X, is handling over 50 short sales at a time.

His acceptance rate on packages is 52.5%, because he is an expert at working with the banks. I am hesitant to release his name and information to my general list of 30,000 plus investors. But, I will allow my Apprentice members to use him on their short sales.

Here's the best part. Mr. X only charges 1.5% of the retail selling price of the house for his services. This is significantly below the 30% to 50% other short sale experts are charging.

And Now Let Me Share With You What Separates My Apprentice Program From Other Normal Run Of The Mill Coaching Programs

FIGURE 5-1. Example of an online, long-form sales letter (continued)

I am sure all of the stuff I've listed above interest you. Anyone can see the value of what is included so far. But is it really that unique?

Are you really getting an Apprenticeship?

If I were to stop right here, I would honestly say NO, you were not getting an apprenticeship. But when you receive the following items, in your Apprenticeship, you'll recognize this is not your run of the mill program.

First of all, being an Apprentice means you and I working together side by side.

It means watching me work, then modeling my processes and work habits to ensure you are successful. It means you get the following...

1. Each and every month, you'll receive not one, but two 20- minute one on one calls with me. We will review deals, discuss strategy, marketing, hit your trouble spots and more. Then....
2. I will personally market for you in your selected area, city and geographic region. That's right, included in the program is me doing the following for you...

   - **I will personally set up** your phone systems, web sites, scripts etc and will pay for them for a full 12 months.
   - **I will personally select** a list of would be sellers, coordinate the mailings, drop your mailings for you and make sure you have the most successful response rates possible off of your marketing. I will do this for up to 2,000 mailers and I will personally pay for this marketing campaign.
   - **I will personally order any signs,** classified ads to get the phone ringing for you. Plus, (you guessed it) I'll pay for all of this as well.
   - **I will personally fly into your town** for one 24 hour period to help you talk with sellers, buyers, realtors, coordinate your business functions and you don't have to pay a penny. I'll even buy you lunch.

Remember, I Am Only Going <u>To Accept 4 People</u> Who We Feel Have What It Takes To Benefit From This Program.

<u>Since you are a member or VIP client, YOU MAY QUALIFY for this program.</u> You'll have the chance to become one of only a chosen few from across the country who will have the privilege of learning from, masterminding with and being coached by myself.

All members that respond to this letter are going to go through an interview process so that I may decide one by one who qualifies and who doesn't. In short, the group will be hand chosen. It has to be that way so that I can insure that I have the best group of real estate investors possible participating in this group.

Let me give you an idea of what this program is all about and what kind of impact it could have on your life...In your six months of Membership...

I Made $57,000 This Month

"I had bought about 15 properties and had made some money investing in real estate, but was not set up to do a lot of volume because my business systems were not well established. I now have a house-buying machine that pumps out between 2 to 4 properties per month. I have systems established in my business that allow me to buy and sell houses via phone and email.

I just flipped a house in March to another investor where I made $27,000 and just closed another deal where I made a total of $57,00 this month."

My best deal ever for quick cash was purchase 112k, repairs of 6k, and sold it the 1st day on the market. I netted 45k in 60 days.

Jonathan Patton, Columbia, SC
College Drop Out

FIGURE 5-1. Example of an online, long-form sales letter (continued)

I Just Do What My Coach Tells Me And I Make Money

"Since in Elite, I've picked up 12 deals in 6 months, all while working full time. I even picked up a property and made $12,000 in one day. Plus I sold another deal and made $37,000. I've just done what Matt tells me to do and made money.

I would recommend Elite coaching to anyone who is serious about real estate. I would invest over and over again for what I've learned."

Steve Gaston - Monroe, NC
Appliance Repair Man

$31,000 In Cash

"Coaching has guided us to success in real estate with encouragement, pushing and pulling with a personal connection. To date we've picked up deals with a total equity of $117,000 and $31,000 in cash.!"

Ken and Diane Stewart Table Rock, SC
Electrician

Coaching Helped Me Make An Additional $109,655.74 On One Deal

"Picked up some very interesting tid-bits to use in my business from the prosperity meeting, I was beginning to get very frustrated with how my business was going, but NOW I'm looking forward to 2005 in a much better light - for not only can I see it happening , I feel it - I BELIEVE... remembering that it's a numbers game - plant the seeds, reap the harvest, by golly I think I've got it!

Oh, here is a check from a deal that I closed while I was attending the event."

- Jackie Coleman - Silver Spring, MD

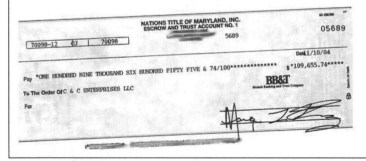

FIGURE 5-1. Example of an online, long-form sales letter (continued)

When I Quit My Job, Even My Boss Was Envious

"We were blaming everyone and everything for not succeeding – but not blaming ourselves.'

Kimberly and I have done four deals since joining the coaching program and have picked up over $100,000 in equity and $25,000 in cash from subject-to deals!! We have two more under contract and several in the pipeline needing just a bit of nuzzling and follow up!"

If you can follow directions, and have faith in your coach then just do it! If they only get one deal out if it they will more than cover the costs. You will learn things that you will never learn from the other gurus.

Matt and Kim Vestrand – Warren, MI
Engineers for General Dynamics

Discover Why A MasterMind Group & An Apprenticeship Are The TRUE Secrets Of Success...

My Apprentice Program incorporates the most powerful, state-of-the-art teaching and learning methods available anywhere in the world today. While allowing you to tap into the power of "The Mastermind", which is incredibly powerful.

Napoleon Hill, author of Think and Grow Rich, made this discovery after years of studying the world's wealthiest and most successful people, 'you need brains besides your own'.

Imagine you will never be alone. Never, be permanently "stuck". We have untied a group of minds that are truly exceptional, like the folks you just read about, at succeeding in real estate and when you join this exceptional group you will discover ways of refining, growing and flourishing in your life and business that you would never have discovered on your own.

Together, I'll help you define your true goals in life,(maybe making more money isn't what will really make you happy, maybe it's having more free time, less stress, a 3 week vacation, tithing more to your church or other causes close to your heart, etc. etc.) We will work as a team to help you define and design a 'life plan' while we continuously 'tweak' and improve every aspect of your personal and professional life, while working less than you have in years.

If the world's best most successful athlete's attribute much of their success to having a great coach, shouldn't you tap into this success "secret" and start working with your own coach to help you reach your business and personal goals as well?

What If The Only Thing Preventing You From Finally Achieving Your Income, Business And Life Goals Is <u>NOT</u> Having A Coach?

You've probably had this experience sometime before,you attend a seminar, read a book, or listened to a tape and felt all fired up with so many phenomenal ideas in your head... ready to change your life! But you soon found yourself overwhelmed to the point of being frozen. Unable to put your new ideas to work, unsure of what direction to take.

Having a coach eliminates this frustration. If you have questions. They are answered. If you need a good "kick in the pants" to get motivated. You've got it.

We will push you to test your limits and achieve far more than you ever thought you were capable of achieving. We'll be there with you, guiding you throughout the year, coaching you to success in every area of your life.

FIGURE 5-1. Example of an online, long-form sales letter (continued)

Can You Put A Price On Your Success?

You've probably assumed by now that there is an investment somewhere along the line for a program this valuable. And, you are right.

What is the cost of this program? It's not cheap. I make no apologies for that. Of course, my own education and expertise has not come cheap either. I've invested hundreds of thousands of dollars to gain my knowledge and continue to invest happily tens of thousands of dollars more learning from the Masters each year. (Why just recently, I invested well over $15,000 including travel to be at a two day event, that recently made me 10 times that amount!)

The investment for this 12 month program is $32,000. Which includes everything you've seen so far in this letter. **But this is a small investment when you remember everything that is included.**

Why just **the cost of me coming into town to spend a day with you is $6,500.00 plus travel expenses**, which can run another $1,500 for first class. For a total of $8,000.00

And to **have me setting up your marketing campaign,** phone systems, paying for the phone system for the 6 months and placing your newspaper ads would **run you over $5,995.00.**

Then, 12 months of coaching with me, for two calls, access to me answering your questions would run you $1,000.00 a month, for a total investment of $6,000.00

Finally is access to my Mr. X to negotiate your short sales. This is PRICELESS! You could not get access to Mr. X, unless you work directly with me.

Heck You'll Spend Twice As Much Just To Attend An Event, Buy More Programs Or Join A Coaching Program That Offers A Quarter Of What I'm Offering You Today!

Think about it. Let's say you attend an event and you pay $3,500.00 to attend. Plus room, food, travel, time away from the family, work, etc. **You are into the event for $5,000.00**

But if at this event, they sell your more programs, phone lines, web sites, coaching programs, you are into this **for another $7,000.00 easily.**

Then you still have to go out market, buy lists, order signs, place classified ads, etc Just to get the phone ringing. **This alone is going to cost you another $5,000.00**

And you still will have to work hard, take time away from the family, work and more. Heck, that's another $2,000.00 in sweat and energy.

This means you are into this for $34,000.00. And you still aren't all the way where you need to be, you still have to learn how to negotiate the short sale, talk with the sellers, figure out how to fill out the paperwork. At this point, you probably would want to call it quits.

I just had a member of mine invest over $100,000.00 with another training company (before they met me) and they didn't get half of what I'm offering you here.

My Apprentice program does all the heavy lifting for you, sends out your marketing pieces, coordinates your system implementation and more. All for less than what is listed above.

Is This Program Guaranteed?

I've been coaching investors for 5 plus years. And here's one thing I've discovered. **You are either 100% committed to making it in real estate or you are not. There are no in betweens. If you need a guarantee, then you are not the right person for this program.** It means you are not ready, you have lingering doubt about yourself and your abilities.

FIGURE 5-1. Example of an online, long-form sales letter (continued)

The program works, **you've seen the success stories.** My track record speaks for it's self. Over 40 million raised in private money by my students, hundreds of millions of dollars in deals done by my members and coaching clients.

Doesn't matter if you are a full time, part time or beginning investor, anyone who is committed who puts 100% into this coaching program will succeed.

Because I give so much of my personal time, energy and resources to the program, I want it to be the most fun, most exhilarating and most profitable program I've ever done. This is a VERY special program. So, not only must I keep the Club limited in size to insure that I give my best attention to it's members, but I must make sure every Apprentice is truly serious about maximizing their success.

Therefore, **I am limiting the membership to 4 total entities.** As of this writing 2 of those spots are taken with existing members or recently initiated members. **There are only 2 spots left to join my Apprentice Program.**

With that in mind, you must show me that you are serious about making changes in your business and your lifestyle by completing and returning the membership application for review.

You must complete this membership form **before at 5 PM Eastern Time**, in order to be eligible for consideration. I will then notify you of a call where we will go into specific detail, answer any and all your questions and you will be able to hear directly from other successful Mastermind Members.

I strongly suggest you take the next step toward success by filling out the application and faxing it or FEDEXing it back to our office. It will then be rushed right into my personal email box. I promise that your journey together in the Apprentice Program will be one of the most satisfying, most rewarding, most profitable and most fun experiences you'll ever have.

<u>Hey, and don't be intimidated if you don't feel like a "success" yet. I'm far more interested in your desire to improve and your willingness to take action to get new results in your life than we are in any past success you have (or haven't) had.</u>

So, if you're serious about FINALLY reaching your goals (or even just defining them), if you're serious about realizing your dreams, and finding that perfect balance between success and peace of mind, then you owe it to yourself to fill out the enclosed membership form and return it to my office immediately, while a spot is still available in this exclusive Club.

To Your Success,

Matthew Gillogly

P.S. How would you like to get your Apprentice Program paid for? Well my entire goal is for you to do a deal. After all you are my Apprentice. And as a Mentor/Apprentice program, it's all about getting real world experience in the real estate business. You and I working together to guide you on the pitfalls of the deal.

That's why I not only want you to do one deal, I want you to do not two, but three deals with me as your partner, (we split the deal 50/50) because with an average profit of $21,536.00 in each deal, you'll easily earn back your investment.

P.P.S. And when we partner on the deals, I will pay you up to $7,000.00 back on each deal from my half. So, we do a short sale together where we net $21,536.00. We split that 50/50. I then pay you back $7,000.00 out of my half for the Apprentice program. Do this on three deals and you net, $53,304.00. That's a 266% return on investment.

FIGURE 5-1. Example of an online, long-form sales letter (continued)

P.P.P.S Due to the importance of this program, I will only accept applications online. You will be notified via email, if you qualify, of the next step. You will receive the information for the private and closed group call, where we will give you all the details on the Apprentice Program. Applications must be received online by 5 PM Eastern in order to be considered for the Apprentice Program.

FIGURE 5-1. Example of an online, long-form sales letter (concluded)

In this sales letter, Matt is selling his apprenticeship program. He offers to partner with real estate investors and teach them how to sell more than they've ever sold before. Everything in the letter is intended to communicate the benefits his readers will receive if they pay to be a part of the program.

Matt's letter contains several subheadlines that set off the sections in which he achieves each of his sales letter's five goals. He begins by describing the problem of making money in a troubled real estate market and then states that coaching programs are the best way to get ahead in the business. He positions himself as the best coach in the business, spends some time justifying the cost of his program and then asks the reader to apply right away.

Matt does a couple of smart things in this letter. He starts by establishing the scarcity of his service—one of the first things you learn is that only four apprentice positions are available. That four-person limit makes his call to action more compelling. He also includes a picture of a six-figure check that one of his former apprentices received—it's a fantastic piece of evidence that goes a long way toward establishing Matt's credibility.

FillMyFunnel.com

The second presentation comes from one of my (Bob Regnerus) websites, **FillMyFunnel.com**. It's an example of a basic multimedia sales presentation (Figure 5-2).

I use this single-page presentation to sell a fairly low-priced item: a set of four CDs, which I value at $197, but which I offer for $12.97 (that's the cost of shipping and handling).

Business Owners - Are You Less Then Happy With The Amount Of Traffic and Sales Coming From Your Website?

Finding It Difficult To Get Time and Expertise In Managing Your Online Marketing Funnel?

In This Free Video, I Will Tell You Exactly Why It Might Be Time To Hire A Traffic and Website Expert, and What You Need To Know About the Person You Are Looking To Hire... No Opt-In Required.

Plus, I Will Send You My Flagship Product "Internet Success Blueprint CDS" FREE (Value $197)...Look For The Offer Below

TheLeadsKing.com©

Thanks For Visiting!

"I look forward to helping you make your website an Income Producing Asset for your business!"

FIGURE 5-2. Example of an online multimedia sales presentation (continued on next page)

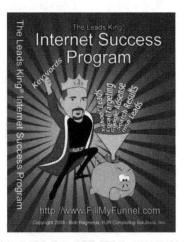

☑ **Yes!** I want to learn more! Please send me your 4-CD Set, The Leads King "Internet Success Blueprint CDS" (Valued at $197) Absolutely FREE without Commitments or Obligations!

Why am I sending you these for free? Simple. I believe that when you hear this information, you will be convinced that I can help you achieve spectacular returns from your website. I know you'll want to work with us and allow us to make you successful. That's why I'm willing to give you a $197 product for free.

I understand the CDs are free and I only need to pay $12.97 for Shipping and Handling

Please click the Order Now Button
To get your Free CD Set by Mail

FIGURE 5-2. Example of an online multimedia sales presentation (continued)

As you can see, the page starts with a large headline that describes the problem I offer to solve: businesses that don't get enough web traffic and have trouble converting leads into customers. There's a slightly smaller (but still easy to read) subheadline that sets the stage for a 20-minute-long slideshow presentation (following).

Ari Galper's ChatWise

CLICK HERE IF you want to say "no thank-you" to the CD offer, but want to know more right now

🔒 **SECURE & CONFIDENTIAL**
Your information will never be rented, traded or sold.
WE GUARANTEE YOUR CONFIDENTIALITY.

TERMS OF USE AND PRIVACY

"Bob is some kind of web site genius!"

"Bob Regnerus is a website genius. I personally recommend him to get you traffic and increase conversions on your website. I have personally used Bob's services, and refer him to my best clients."

Bill Glazer, president of the exclusive Kennedy/Glazer newsletter and the foremost authority on marketing for retail stores in North America, routinely refers Bob to his best clients for online traffic and online marketing strategies. Bill recently invited him to speak at the exclusive Information Marketer's Summit in Dallas, TX.

FIGURE 5-2. Example of an online multimedia sales presentation (continued)

"...what separates you from everyone else is..."

"Bob - anyone can drive traffic to a website. What separates you from everyone else is that you helped me make more money through my website. That one change you recommended turned the webpage from 11.56% conversion to 24.7% overnight!. Sheer genius!"

Matt Gillogly
Real Estate Coach and Mentor
http://www.createtruerriches.com

"My entire office is in an uproar
over the increase in signups!"

"Hey Bob, You have really impressed me with your Google skills. My entire office is in an uproar over the increase in signups!"

April 28 - "Bob - I just filled my 300 seat event, entirely off the leads you produced for me. That's impressive!"

Mark Sumpter
Real Estate Coach and Mentor
http://www.marksumpterlive.com

FIGURE 5-2. Example of an online multimedia sales presentation (continued)

"...Thanks for the fantastic ideas on improving my landing page..."

"You cannot believe how much of a relief it is to have someone like you helping me fill my online marketing funnel. I don't have the time to do it and we've been delaying it for so long. Thanks for the fantastic ideas on improving my landing page and helping us steer around the infamous "Google Slap!"

Alexandria K. Brown, a.k.a. "The Ezine Queen" & Million Dollar Marketing Coach to Solo-preneurs Around the World
http://www.ezinequeen.com

☑ **Yes!** I want to learn more! Please send me your 4-CD Set, The Leads King "Internet Success Blueprint CDS" (Valued at $197) Absolutely FREE without Commitments or Obligations!

FIGURE 5-2. Example of an online multimedia sales presentation (continued)

I understand the CDs are free and I only need to pay
$12.97 for Shipping and Handling

Please click the Order Now Button
To get your Free CD Set by Mail

**CLICK HERE IF you want to say "no thank-you" to the CDs
offer, but want to know more right now**

🔒 SECURE & CONFIDENTIAL
Your information will never be rented, traded or sold.
WE GUARANTEE YOUR CONFIDENTIALITY.

TERMS OF USE AND PRIVACY

"...$2,351 per day traffic strategy!..."

"Bob is an Internet superstar. He personally
developed a complete Internet strategy for my company
that at it's peak, generated $2,351 in a single day.
This strategy and technical plan Bob created for me
was responsible for over $470,377 dollars in profits
to me last year.

Since then, I've personally worked with Bob on many
projects for clients and have witnessed how much he's
able to turn their websites upside-down and create
smokin' direct response websites that generate more
leads for less money.

I cannot recommend him enough - I continue to refer
new clients to him weekly, and drop everything I'm
doing to work with him when something new comes
along!"

Bill Bodri, a.k.a. "The Million Dollar USP Man"
http://www.uspnichemarketing.com/

FIGURE 5-2. Example of an online multimedia sales presentation
(continued)

Copyright RJR Computing Solutions, Inc.
PO Box 251
Palos Heights, IL 60463
Phone 1-877-349-2615

CLICK HERE IF you want to say "no thank-you" to the CDs
offer, but want to know more right now

FIGURE 5-2. Example of an online multimedia sales presentation (concluded)

In the slideshow, I spend 10 minutes describing the problem in detail, and then I describe the solution: hiring an expert to handle web traffic and sales conversion. I give some basic pointers on choosing an expert, and then I present myself as the obvious choice and ask the viewer to order my CD set, which will provide even more information.

It's easy to justify the price of those CDs because they're essentially free. I follow up the slideshow with a call to action—"Please Click the Order Now Button to Get Your Free CD Set by Mail"—and then I provide several testimonials to establish my credibility.

I repeat the call to action again, lower on the page, so my sales leads don't have to scroll up after they go through the testimonials. At the bottom of the page, I provide my contact information and some credentials, such as my certifications in the Google and Yahoo! pay-per-click advertising systems.

Model #2: The Tele-Seminar

A tele-seminar is a sales presentation delivered over the phone, usually in the form of a conference call. You can conduct the seminar live and in real time, or you can record the seminar in advance and play it at the scheduled time. If you use a tele-seminar as your sales presentation, you should schedule at least one per week, preferably two. Try to get your new sales leads to participate in the next scheduled call after they opt in on your landing page.

An effective tele-seminar follows the same five-point outline as an online sales presentation: describe the problem, identify the solution, separate yourself from the competition, justify your price, inspire immediate action. The only difference is the delivery method.

Telephone sales presentations aren't right for every information marketing business, but when used appropriately, they have several advantages over online sales presentations:

Personal touch. Phone conversations, even if they're one-way, seem more casual and personal, so they're better at establishing a connection between you and your sales leads. Online sales presentations can do a decent job of it, especially when they include video content, but telephone contact is still the next best thing to a face-to-face conversation.

Defined timing. You can't be sure that you'll have your sales leads' full attention when they see an online sales presentation. They may have stumbled across your website and decided to opt in while they were eating lunch, talking on the phone or killing time between meetings. If something else is happening at the same time, they may just glance at the screen occasionally while your presentation is running.

Tele-seminars, on the other hand, take place at a defined date and time, so your participants can plan ahead. Most of them will have cleared that time on their schedules, so you'll contend with fewer distractions.

Also, you control the timing of a tele-seminar. Your sales leads don't have the option of skipping over a section they don't think will be important or jumping ahead to get a look at the price. Your sales presentation will be most effective when you can walk your leads through each of the five steps in their proper order, and a tele-seminar makes it easier to do that.

Duration. Tele-seminars can vary in length from 15 minutes to two hours, but even at the low end of that range, they're longer than a typical online sales presentation. That gives you the opportunity to present more information and repeat your key points several times, without sounding like a broken record.

Does the additional length mean that your participants might be doing other things while they're on the call? Sometimes, but don't worry. If you can keep someone on the phone for an hour or more, you'll get plenty of information across, no matter what else is going on in the background.

Flexibility. Changing or updating an online sales presentation isn't the most difficult thing in the world, but it takes at least a little bit of time, and if you outsource your web administration, it'll cost you at least a little bit of money. Tele-seminars are much easier to change. If you use a recorded seminar, you can record new material whenever you have it and splice it into the existing recording. If you do your seminars live, it's just a matter of changing your notes before the call.

When to use a tele-seminar. Since they take place outside your website, tele-seminars are better suited to higher-priced products or services—the ones your sales leads will need time to think about before they decide to buy.

Tele-seminars are particularly good for selling coaching and consulting services. The personal connection and extended length can do a lot to make your leads feel comfortable with you, and that's one of the most important elements in the sales process.

You can use your tele-seminar as your landing page offer, or you can include it as a surprise bonus for prospects who opt in for a different offer. Figure 5-3 (page 118) shows a good example of a site that uses a tele-seminar as a special bonus.

Visitors to this page have opted in by clicking a link to receive a free report from Bill Glazer. After clicking that link, they are taken to

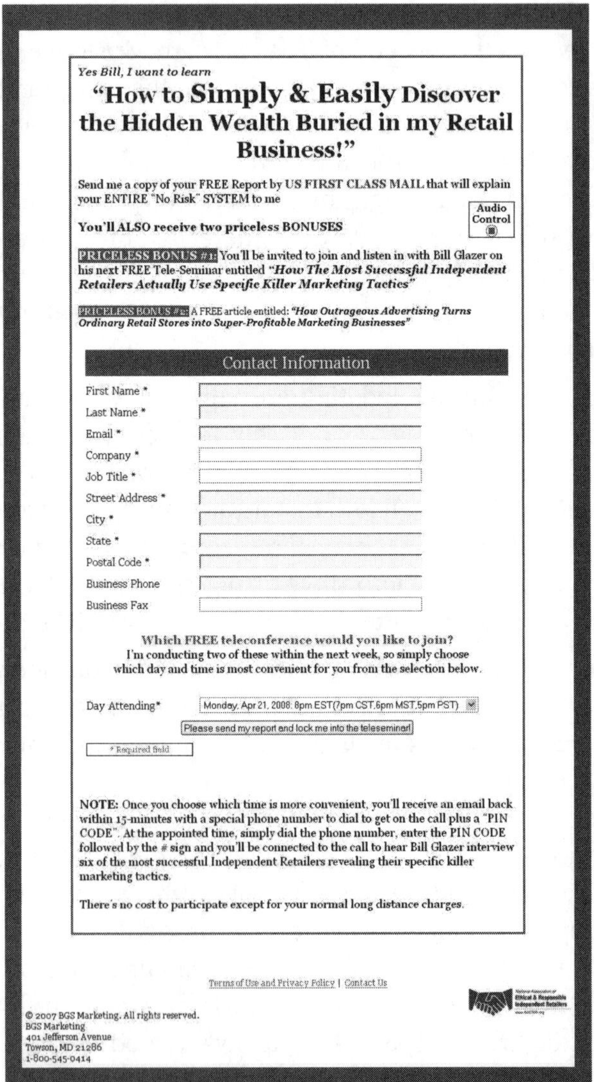

Yes Bill, I want to learn

"How to Simply & Easily Discover the Hidden Wealth Buried in my Retail Business!"

Send me a copy of your FREE Report by US FIRST CLASS MAIL that will explain your ENTIRE "No Risk" SYSTEM to me

Audio Control

You'll ALSO receive two priceless BONUSES

PRICELESS BONUS #1: You'll be invited to join and listen in with Bill Glazer on his next FREE Tele-Seminar entitled ***"How The Most Successful Independent Retailers Actually Use Specific Killer Marketing Tactics"***

PRICELESS BONUS #2: A FREE article entitled: ***"How Outrageous Advertising Turns Ordinary Retail Stores into Super-Profitable Marketing Businesses"***

Contact Information

First Name *
Last Name *
Email *
Company *
Job Title *
Street Address *
City *
State *
Postal Code *
Business Phone
Business Fax

Which FREE teleconference would you like to join?
I'm conducting two of these within the next week, so simply choose which day and time is most convenient for you from the selection below.

Day Attending* Monday, Apr 21, 2008: 8pm EST(7pm CST,6pm MST,5pm PST)

Please send my report and lock me into the teleseminar!

* Required field

NOTE: Once you choose which time is more convenient, you'll receive an email back within 15-minutes with a special phone number to dial to get on the call plus a "PIN CODE". At the appointed time, simply dial the phone number, enter the PIN CODE followed by the # sign and you'll be connected to the call to hear Bill Glazer interview six of the most successful Independent Retailers revealing their specific killer marketing tactics.

There's no cost to participate except for your normal long distance charges.

Terms of Use and Privacy Policy | Contact Us

© 2007 BGS Marketing. All rights reserved.
BGS Marketing
401 Jefferson Avenue
Towson, MD 21286
1-800-545-0414

FIGURE 5-3. Example of offering a tele-seminar on a landing page this page, which collects their mailing addresses and announces the bonus tele-seminar. At the bottom of the page, the visitor chooses a seminar date (there are always two calls to choose from in the next week) and gets information about the confirmation e-mails that will follow.

Delivering your tele-seminar. There are two delivery options for your tele-seminar: you can do it live, or you can record it ahead of time.

Whichever delivery method you choose, be sure to send your participants several follow-up e-mails in the days leading up to the call. If your sales leads will be waiting five or six days between opting in and hearing your tele-seminar, there's a definite risk that they'll forget the call-in details. Play it safe and remind them.

Live tele-seminars. The main advantage to doing your tele-seminar live is that you can set aside time for a question-and-answer session after you've completed your presentation. This personal interaction will help build a personal connection with your sales leads.

Live delivery also keeps your material fresh and gives you the option to include guest speakers any time you find someone who has the time to participate and whose opinion will matter to your sales leads.

Prerecorded tele-seminars. The downside of live tele-seminar delivery is that you have to be on the phone for one or two hours, once or twice a week. If you don't have the time to do a live tele-seminar, record it ahead of time and use a tele-seminar service to play the recording when your participants are on the line.

Recording your tele-seminars gives you the opportunity to use this type of sales presentation in several marketing campaigns at the same time. No one has the time to conduct two or three live seminars every day, but with a series of recorded tele-seminars, you can maintain that schedule seven days a week and not lose a minute of your time.

Model #3: The Shock-and-Awe Package

Dan Kennedy, one of the world's most successful marketers, first introduced us to the Shock-and-Awe sales presentation. It's a great way to make an impression on your sales leads when you're selling high-priced products or services.

The Shock-and-Awe package takes its name from a well-known military strategy. When the American-led coalition invaded Iraq in 2003, Secretary of Defense Donald Rumsfeld described the invasion as a "Shock-and-Awe" operation that would overwhelm the enemy with a massive display of power. By using almost every type of weapon in its arsenal in a coordinated assault, the coalition defeated the Iraqi army in a matter of days.

When used in a sales campaign, a Shock-and-Awe package overwhelms the recipient with an array of impressive materials and convincing arguments. Anyone who gets a Shock-and-Awe package delivered to his or her home will have to sit up and take notice.

A typical Shock-and-Awe package arrives in a large box, usually delivered by a courier or overnight delivery service. It might weigh over 25 pounds, and it will include a massive amount of high-quality information. Here's a list of materials you might want to include in a Shock-and-Awe package:

- A sales letter that summarizes your offer and describes the rest of the materials in the package.
- DVDs containing multimedia sales presentations and/or video recordings of your live sales presentations. High-end Shock-and-Awe packages might even include a portable DVD player with the DVD loaded inside.
- CDs containing audio content (recorded interviews or teleseminars, for example), trial software or electronic versions of the printed materials in the Shock-and-Awe box.
- Copies of articles written by you or about you.

- Copies of books you've written.
- Binders filled with customer testimonials and case studies.

When to use a Shock-and-Awe package. Shock-and-Awe packages aren't cheap, and the biggest ones can cost over $100 to prepare and ship. Obviously, this is only something you'll want to do if you're selling products or services with price tags in the thousands.

Delivering a Shock-and-Awe package. You've spent a lot of money on your Shock-and-Awe package, so give it the priority it deserves and send it overnight express. Your sales leads are considering spending a lot of money on your product or service, and they'll appreciate the interest you show by getting your package to them right away.

If you have the time, you might even want to make a personal call to your sales lead to confirm that the package was delivered.

Beth Davis Carries Her Business Map in Her Hands

Info-Marketer Profile

Beth Davis has a unique mission in life: She trains people to implement their own life missions by reading and understanding their hands, commonly known as "palm reading" or hand analysis.

"In 1999, I started my business of doing one-on-one hand-analysis sessions," Beth says. "I realized I could make more money doing that than working at my corporate job because people were willing to pay me $100 an hour. At the time, $100 was staggering to me—and it still is for a lot of people who don't understand information marketing." Today, Beth charges $497 per session and is poised to raise her rates.

Beth began her career in the corporate world of marketing. She worked for a museum design firm, and her job was to respond to leads, help develop proposals and pitch prospective clients. "I actually left that job," Beth says, "because my boss wouldn't let me ➡

work on commission. I was finding very lucrative multimillion-dollar projects, and I said to my boss, 'If you let me work purely on commission, you don't even have to pay me a salary. Just let me work on commission for 5 percent.' And he said, 'Well, I can't have you making more money than me.' Then I said, 'Well, I can't work here anymore.'"

Actually, Beth used her presentation skills to pitch a well-thought-out presentation with graphics depicting her increasing responsibilities over time contrasted with her flat line of income growth with the company. "I said, 'You see the discrepancy here?' He laughed and said, 'That was a really great presentation, but my answer's no.'"

To add insult to injury, Beth's boss added, "And you'll be lucky if you're making $40,000 a year in five years."

That was all the motivation Beth needed to give her notice and open her own business. But how did marketing lead to hand analysis? Beth explains: "The hand reading was really a hobby. I had been very stuck in my own life, and a friend kept urging me to do this particular type of hand analysis. I told her I didn't believe in that stuff, and I didn't want to do it … I was open-minded, but it just seemed kind of ridiculous to me, honestly."

All that changed for Beth when she went for a hand analysis of her own. "This woman read my hands and basically told me that I would be doing what I'm doing now—that my life's purpose was to be a successful business owner who inspires the masses."

Beth started teaching hand analysis by phone in 2002. "My very first tele-class, I enrolled 10 people at $500 a person. I made $5,000 for this short tele-class, and I went, 'Oh, hot diggity-dog. This works!'" Beth remembers. "A number of those people went on to become professional hand analysts as a result."

➡️

As Beth continued to build her business, she subscribed to Alexandria Brown's e-zine (**AlexandriaBrown.com**). "I saw that every time Ali sent out an e-mail, she made a bunch of money," Beth says. "That intrigued me. And so I thought, 'I gotta figure out how to take my website from a floating brochure to another revenue stream for my business.' I didn't know how to do that. I knew I had the tele-classes, and I knew I could do hand readings by phone."

The internet was a natural solution for Beth because she was living in a secluded area of the country. "I mean it was so remote, the nearest grocery store was an hour and 15 minutes away!" she laughs. "All I had was a telephone and a dial-up internet connection."

Beth began sending plain text e-mails to her list of 600 people, and it worked. People enrolled in her tele-classes and workshops, and that allowed her to sell more hand readings. It was also in 2002 that she began her coaching program. "I knew I had to make a continuity income," she says, "and I was aware that I did have this skill as a coach. I knew I could help people get results. So, I started up-selling people into a six-month coaching program at the end of the hand readings. I was very clear that it was an up-sell. I didn't advertise the coaching anywhere because I didn't want people contacting me about coaching. I wanted to choose who I worked with, so I never advertised it. Within six to eight months, I had a full practice."

The next big step came in the summer of 2005, when Beth signed up for Alexandria Brown's "Online Success Blueprint Workshop." "I got home from the workshop, and I pretty much implemented everything she said to do," Beth says. "I sent out a survey to my list to see what my customers wanted most, and about 600 people responded. Half the people wanted to learn about

➡

their hand information as it related to their business, and the other half actually wanted to learn about the hand information itself."

Then Beth hired a web designer to build her new website, **HandAnalyst.com**, with an opt-in box in the upper right corner of the web page—the place Ali told her to put it for the most opt-ins. Based on research Beth did on her target market, she decided to focus on women. The site offers a free report entitled "The Five Massive Mistakes Spiritually-Oriented Women Make in Business (… *and how to avoid them!*)."

Beth's first information product was a home study program called "How to Read Your Own Hands: 5 Proven Steps to Bring More Health, Love and Money Into Your Life." It teaches people the benefits of analyzing their own hands and sells for $247. "Those are most people's physical considerations—health, love and money," Beth says. "The title basically encompasses all of the responses I got on the survey. Half the group cares about experience and process. They don't care about buying a bigger car or a flat-screen TV. What they want is a really juicy soul-altering experience. And then there's another group that's very interested in the results and the bottom line."

Chapter 6

King Consummation

The Only Way to Get the Sale Is to Ask for It

KING CONSUMMATION IS THE KING OF CLOSING THE DEAL. HE walks alongside wanderers who are ready to take the final steps of their journeys and ensures they know exactly what they're doing. Without his help, many wanderers would have doubts at the last minute and flee the kingdom before achieving their objectives. Those others who enter the kingdom without speaking to King Salutation and King Presentation would never know what they were missing.

Your online order form should do for your website what King Consummation does for his kingdom. It should ensure that customers know what they are getting and what they have to pay to get it. It should provide additional encouragement to customers who need a push before they hit the "Submit Payment" button. It should summarize the key points of your sales presentation, in case your visitor skimmed over it or skipped it entirely. A well-designed order form prevents lost sales and turns casual visits into sales opportunities.

It's important to remember that online order forms are not only for online stores. Even if you're selling consulting services or coaching programs that cost tens of thousands of dollars, you may want to put an order form on your website.

If your business model starts with generating leads on your website and then following up with phone calls and printed materials, you still need a way to complete the process when your leads are ready to become customers. Very few information marketers have storefronts with clerks and cash registers, so how do you collect the money? The mail is slow, phone sales are a hassle, and faxes are unreliable and vulnerable to information theft. An online order form is the most convenient way to complete a sale, both for the buyer and the seller.

Yes, You Really Do Have to Ask for It

Despite the obvious importance of the ordering process, most businesses neglect it. Even very smart business owners, people who spend lots of time and money perfecting their landing pages and sales presentations, make this mistake. They assume visitors will be so blown away by what they've seen that they'll be ready to pay as soon as the next page opens. Unfortunately, it doesn't work that way. When visitors look at your online order form, it simply means they're still interested and want to see the bottom line. Your order form needs to play an active part in the process to ensure that you close as many sales as possible.

It only takes the click of a mouse (if that) to open your order form after the end of your sales presentation, so don't assume that everyone who gets to that point is fully engaged. Many visitors will still be looking for answers when they get to your order form. You need to provide them with more than a space to enter their credit card numbers. When you provide useful information, focusing on the benefits of your product or service, you'll win over many of those undecided consumers.

Remember that some casual visitors will look at your order form simply out of curiosity. They may not intend to buy anything; they may not have paid attention during the presentation. Still, there's a chance that something on your order form may catch their eye, and there's no reason to pass up the opportunity. You only have to build your order form once, and it will go to work for you every time it opens.

On the other hand, even the most interested, most attentive visitor is bound to miss a few of the points you make in your sales presentation. External distractions or technical difficulties can easily take visitors away for 5 or 10 seconds—not so long that most people would go back to find out what they missed, but long enough to miss one fact or idea that would have sealed the deal.

You can't repeat your entire presentation on your order form, but you can—and should—repeat the highlights. You'll reinforce the key selling points in every visitor's mind, and you'll give yourself a second chance with the ones who missed something important.

The Rogue Visitor

There's something else to consider here: the rogue visitor.

Not every visitor who opens your order page is getting to it the way you intend. Some of them will opt in on your landing page without reading a word, and click through your presentation as quickly as their browser allows. Others will go to your order page without seeing anything else on your site because a friend recommended your product or service and e-mailed them a direct link to that page. This can also happen if someone finds a direct link on a search engine results page.

Some of these rogue visitors are rushing to your order form because they can't wait to make a purchase. Maybe they're existing customers who buy everything you offer, or maybe they're impulsive. Either way, your order form still has some work to do. It needs to confirm to these customers that they're actually buying what they think they're buying, and it needs to keep them excited about what they're doing. Even the most enthusiastic customer can be turned off by an indifferent order page.

The other group of unconventional visitors are the ones who only want to see what your product or service will cost. One way or another, they'll skip past everything that gets between them and the price tag. The price should be easy to see on your order form, obviously, but it should be placed in a context that allows visitors to see the value of what you're offering. These people might not know anything about you or your business, and they may not go back and start at the beginning. Your order form is your one chance to state your case to these visitors, so you had better take advantage of the opportunity.

When in doubt, design your order page with these renegade visitors in mind. You won't drive a typical visitor away by putting in some extra effort, but if you take shortcuts, you'll lose opportunities with the visitors who come in for a quick look. Think about everyone who will look at this page, and follow King Consummation's seven laws for effective online order forms.

> For other unique ways to capture and process orders from customers, visit **InternetInfoMarketing Book.com/orders**.

King Consummation's Seven Laws for Effective Order Forms

Law #1: Use a Benefit-Driven Headline

Let's start at the top. Your order form needs a headline. If you think that sounds silly or unnecessary, you need to change the way you think about your order form. It's not just a web page that performs a transaction. It's one of the critical parts of your sales machine.

While it's true that some visitors have already decided to make a purchase by the time they get to your order page, most are still on the fence. Your order form is your last chance to get them on your side of that fence. When they finish reading the page, they are either going to go through with the purchase, or they are going to click away and look at someone else's website. Your order form has to do everything possible to achieve the sale, and that starts with a good headline.

A good order page headline is like a good landing page headline or sales letter headline. It should describe the problem that your product or service will solve, and it should spur the visitor to immediate action. We don't recommend reusing one of your other headlines on your order page because your visitors will feel they've already responded to it. It's OK if some of your headlines are similar—just don't repeat them word for word.

Whether visitors go through your sales presentation or jump right to your order form, you need to grab their attention and get them excited about your offer. Most of them are viewing the page out of curiosity, so if you greet them with something more than a price tag, they'll be surprised and feel compelled to keep reading. Since you're going to follow your headline with a detailed list of what's included in the product or service you're offering, you'll keep your visitors' attention. And since you're going to discuss the benefits of each element of the offer, you'll greatly improve your chances of closing the sale.

To determine the effectiveness of a headline, try something we learned from Dan Kennedy. Dan puts every headline to his "Classified Ad Test." If you could publish your headline in the newspaper as a classified ad and get responses, it's a good headline. If it doesn't provide enough detail or excitement to work as a classified ad, it won't work as a headline, either. Use this test on every headline you write, including the headline for your order form.

Law #2: State the Benefits

Your order form should list the benefits your customers will gain by completing their orders. This is ground you've already covered in your sales presentation, but you can't assume that your visitors remember everything they saw or that they saw everything you wanted them to.

Here's a great trick for getting customers engaged in the process and stating your benefits at the same time: turn the order form around and write it as though it's coming from the customer's point of view. We use this technique on many of our own order forms. Rather than saying "Complete this form to receive the new 8-DVD information kit from Bob Regnerus," for example, Bob's order form would say, "Yes! Send me the new 8-DVD information kit from Bob Regnerus, which will give me step-by-step instructions for generating sales leads online!"

As with almost everything on your website, you have to find a middle ground between providing too little information and providing too much. You don't want to omit the one sentence that would convince a visitor to become a customer, but you don't want to include so much text that the order form becomes cluttered, confusing or overly long. Putting obstacles in the way of a motivated buyer is just as bad as neglecting a hesitant buyer.

Law #3: State the Deliverable

Your order form must ensure that your customers know what they're paying for. You've already given a complete description of your product or service in your sales presentation, but you should repeat the key points here as well.

Many customers get distracted during a sales presentation, even when they're interested in making a purchase. They may fail to understand something in your presentation, or they may be too excited to pay close attention. If they expect one thing and receive something else, you have a customer service problem on your hands. At best, you or someone on your staff will have to take a call or an e-mail from the customer and provide an explanation. At worst, you'll have to give the customer a refund.

A good order form eliminates these problems by describing, in detail, every aspect of the product or service being offered.

This is another opportunity to state the benefits of your product or service. You might even want to combine the two steps and describe the benefits of each deliverable as you list them.

In addition to listing the items or services your customers will receive, you should describe exactly how they'll be delivered. Is the customer buying an e-book or other item that will be available for immediate download? Describe the download process. Is your customer buying a set of books, binders or DVDs? Describe the materials and the packaging they will come in. Is your customer buying a place in a seminar or a conference? Give the time and date, and describe the confirmation you'll send later.

Tell your customer whether you use FedEx, UPS or the USPS to deliver your products, and tell them how long it will take for the delivery to arrive. If you use a traceable delivery method, mention that the customer will get a tracking number after the order has been processed.

All this may sound like overkill, but the more detail you provide now, the less time you'll spend dealing with customers who are surprised by what they receive.

Law #4: Offer Choices and Terms

Your order form is one of the few places on your website where it's a good idea to offer more than a simple yes-or-no decision. By offering different versions of your product or service or different payment terms, you'll increase your revenue and help some of your customers overcome concerns about your price.

Here's a simple trick that's almost guaranteed to increase your profits: Offer a deluxe version of whatever you're selling.

A certain percentage of consumers (some studies have shown that it's as large as 20 percent) will choose the more expensive version of a product or a service every time they're offered the choice. So, no matter what you're selling, even if you haven't presented separate versions of it in your sales materials, give your order page visitors the chance to buy the deluxe edition.

Don't have a deluxe edition? Don't worry. Creating it will take almost no time at all. As long as you have more than one product or service, all you have to do is bundle a few of them and call it the "Gold Package." This could be any combination: an e-book and a membership site subscription or a coaching program and a seminar registration or a membership site subscription and a seminar registration. As long as they address related topics and are likely to appeal to the same type of customer, they'll work as a package.

You may also want to offer different payment options or terms. If you're selling a monthly subscription service, you can give your customers the option to pay up front for a full year in return for a 10 percent discount. You can also go the other way and offer an installment plan for large purchases, in return for a 10 percent premium.

Either way, your flexibility on the terms of payment will work to your advantage. Customers with money to spend will be happy to take advantage of your upfront discount, and customers who are short on cash will gladly pay a higher total price if they can spread out the payments.

Law #5: Re-Establish Your Credibility

Even though you've provided evidence of your trustworthiness on your landing page and in your sales presentation, you have to do it again on your order form. Some of your order form visitors will need a little extra encouragement to make the jump from sales lead to customer. They're worried that they're about to do something rash. They need reassurance that many other people have done the same thing before them and that those people have been happy with the result. Provide a few more customer testimonials on your order form to help your nervous leads overcome their fears.

This is an area where you have to think of your rogue visitors—the ones who haven't seen or paid attention to your landing page and sales presentation. They didn't see all the evidence you provided earlier in the sales process, so this is your only chance to show them you're a legitimate business. In addition to your testimonials, include the other basic tools for establishing credibility: your memberships and certifications, your privacy policy and your contact information.

Order Processing. One thing you must do to gain your customers' trust is provide a secure order processing system. The next time you submit personal information on a website—say, when you're buying something from an online merchant or checking your bank account balance—look at the web address at the top of your browser window. You'll: see that the "http" prefix before the web address changes to "https" when you open a page that uses your personal info. That extra *s* stands for "secure," and it shows up when you're on a page that uses strong encryption to protect your information. This is something you'll want to do on your own website's order form. We've seen many beginning information marketers try to collect credit card numbers on unsecured sites, and it just doesn't work. Technically savvy customers will notice if you're not using secure encryption, and many of your customers' security programs won't let them submit orders on unsecured sites, even if they want to.

Tell your web administrator that you need 128-bit encryption on your order form, or use an outside vendor like 1ShoppingCart (**TheLeadsKingShoppingCart.com**) or Infusion Software (**TheLeads KingCRM.com**), which will handle secure payment processing for you.

Law #6: Remove Risk

As Dan Kennedy says, if you can't guarantee what you sell, sell something else. A guarantee is essential for closing sales on the internet. That's just as true for information marketers as it is for everyone else—if anything, it's more important.

Look at this from your customers' point of view, and try to imagine the uncertainty they'll experience when they first see your order form. There's a lot at stake at that moment, especially when you're selling more expensive products or services.

On one hand, your customers are anxious to solve the problem that led them to your website in the first place. They've seen your sales materials, they've decided that you might have the right solution for them, and they want to see the information you're selling.

On the other hand, your customers have no firsthand experience with you. Your sales materials are attractive, and you've provided plenty of convincing testimonials, but how can they really know that you're trustworthy? They've made bad purchases before (who hasn't?), and they don't want to make that mistake again. If they're considering spending thousands of dollars, they may need to justify the purchase to their husband or wife, their employer or a board of directors. At the very least, they want to avoid the embarrassment of being taken for a ride.

So, how do you overcome these fears and objections? Offer a money-back guarantee. The stronger your guarantee and the longer it stays valid, the more effective it will be. An iron-clad guarantee makes you appear more confident in your product or service, and it removes almost all the last-minute concerns a potential customer might have.

Some people will buy from you simply because you offer a guarantee—they figure that there's no risk involved, so they may as well find out what you have to offer.

Don't lose sleep over the money you will potentially have to pay back to your customers. Very few people take advantage of money-back guarantees. Some people will actually make a purchase with the intention of demanding their money back, but in most cases, they won't follow through. If you find that you're paying money back to a large percentage of your customers, it means there's something seriously wrong with your product or service.

As long as you're not running a scam operation, you have little to lose and a great deal to gain by offering a money-back guarantee. Removing risk on your order form will result in higher sales. Guaranteed.

Law #7: Provide Instructions

Providing detailed, step-by-step instructions is important in every phase of your sales process, but your order form is where you really have to go all out. If anything about your order form is confusing or unclear, your customers will get frustrated and decide to buy from one of your competitors instead.

This is where another short video presentation can come in handy. Think about adding a quick (one minute or less) video in which you thank your visitors for deciding to make a purchase, repeat the key benefits of your product or service, and give instructions for filling out the order form.

Whether you give your instructions in a video or in text, be specific. Tell your sales leads that they need to choose between the basic package and the Gold Package, tell them to provide complete information in every space on the form, and remind them to include their payment information. Point out things like the location of the three-digit security code on the back of your customers' credit cards. Even if they've made hundreds of online purchases before, they may need a gentle nudge at certain points in the process.

The Help Line

Giving your customers access to a toll-free help line is a great way to avoid lost sales on your order form. Some customers will need to be guided through every step of the order process, no matter how good your instructions are. Others will feel more comfortable speaking to a human being when they place their orders.

This is something many information marketers leave off their order forms, often because they lack the time or resources to provide 24-hour customer service by phone. It's not a must-have, but if you can do it, the phone support will probably pay for itself several times over.

Special Bonus: The Thank-You Page

After your customers place their orders, what do you do with them? You can't just leave them on the order page, or they'll think something went wrong. The best solution is to take them to a "thank-you" page once the order has been processed.

Your customers have just taken a leap of faith by buying something from you, and they'll appreciate it if you take a moment to acknowledge the fact. After you thank them for their business, take one last opportunity to list the products or services you'll be delivering and state the benefits of each item. Reassure your customers that the order has been completed successfully, and let them know what's going to happen next. Will they get an e-mail with a FedEx tracking code? If so, when will they get it? This is a good way to avoid customer service inquiries in the future.

You can also use your thank-you page to start a new sales process. You've built up some momentum, and you've convinced your customers that it's safe to do business with you, so why not offer an additional product or service? One way to do this without seeming pushy is to throw in a special bonus, like a free report or a seminar registration, which will kick off another sales presentation.

Sample Order Form

The order form for membership in Robert Skrob's Information Marketing Association is a perfect example of an effective online order form. To see it, go to **https://m344. infusionsoft.com/sale-form/nifhnat**.

> To easily add ordering and payment functions to your online marketing process, use the solution Bob Regnerus routinely recommends to clients at **TheLeadsKingShopping Cart.com.**

This form starts with a large, benefit-driven headline, which explains what is being offered even to people who haven't seen any of the pages that led to the order form.

Next, there's a clever feature: The form sums up the entire ordering process, including a review of the deliverables, the cost and the terms of the purchase, in one simple paragraph at the top of the form. It's all phrased from the customer's point of view:

> Yes, Robert, I want to join the Information Marketing Association, receive the monthly trade journal, Dan Kennedy's NO BS Info-Letter/Information Marketing Special Reports, monthly Best Practices tele-seminar, monthly Jumpstart coaching call and so much more. I agree to abide by the Code of Ethics. Please bill my credit card for my membership dues of $99.00 per month. I understand that I may cancel at any time with a simple fax request. (Dues for international members outside the USA are $109.00 per month.)

You can't be much more upfront than that.

Below that summary, the form provides a detailed and convincing list of deliverables and the benefits of each. There's a prominent money-back guarantee followed by detailed instructions for completing the form and submitting payment information.

Notice that the form at the web page referred to above provides the logos of the credit cards accepted by the IMA and points out where customers can find that magic three-digit security code. Robert also gives his customers the option to submit their orders by fax or mail if they prefer—that's something to consider doing on your own order form.

The form itself, where customers provide their personal information and payment information, is simple and easy to read, and it concludes with another statement from the customer's point of view, this time to confirm all the terms of the purchasing agreement.

If your own online order form looks like this one, you're getting it right.

Building an Info-Business in 27 Minutes a Week

Info-Marketer Profile

Robert W. Bly is a newcomer to the information marketing industry, but chances are you have seen his work in print—and you may even know his name.

Before putting his own information product online just a year or so ago, Bob spent 25 years as a freelance direct response copywriter. His clients include Agora Publishing, Rodale, AARP, American Writers and Artists Institute and dozens of newsletter publishers, technology companies, financial services and health care companies.

He is also the author of more than 70 traditionally published books. His best known book is *The Copywriters Handbook*, published in 1985 by Henry Hope, and he has written on a wide variety of other topics.

"A lot of them have been on business and marketing topics," Bob says, "and communications and writing. For example, I wrote a best-selling business-writing book called *The Elements of Business Writing*. But I've done other things. I've written a book on sex. I've ➡

written a book on *Star Trek*. I've written books on careers and computers. I've written a book on Stephen King. I've written a humor book called the *I Hate Kathie Lee Gifford Book*. So, I've done a lot of different stuff."

While the books about *Star Trek*, Kathie Lee and Stephen King were more fun to write, Bob's books on copywriting and business writing are what launched his career. "My first book, *The Elements of Technical Writing*, accelerated my career and was my means of establishing myself in advertising," Bob says. "Other people could run ads, give speeches or network at direct marketing association functions, but I wrote books."

Traditional wisdom might argue against the value of writing books. Some beginning info-marketers believe if you put everything you know in a book and teach readers what to do, they won't need to hire you. Bob disagrees. "No, it's the complete opposite. What happens is when you write a book or an article or an information product, people listen to it and say, 'Boy, this guy knows what he's doing,' and 'Boy, that's a lot of work; I don't want to do that. I'll hire him to do it.'"

So, why would a successful published author "jump ship" into information marketing? Bob explains: "The book publishing industry is an industry with problems. A lot of people seek to have a 'book-book' published because there's a status to it. But I've had that experience over 70 times. It doesn't do anything for me anymore."

Encouraged by friends and colleagues in the publishing business—including University Publishers, Johns Hopkins University and Harvard—Bob decided to try selling his books on the internet.

At first, Bob was hesitant. "I remember telling people, 'I'm really happy doing what I'm doing, and I'm so busy. Between copywriting and writing books, I work 12 hours a day,'" Bob recalls. "I also ➡

stayed away from internet marketing because I viewed it as too detail-oriented. I'm not a detail person. It seemed like the technical parts were beyond me. Plus, I envisioned myself having to wrap up books in my bedroom and then mailing them out myself. I didn't want to do that, so I stayed away from the internet."

Midlife finally nudged Bob forward. "About a year ago, I woke up one day and thought, 'I'm almost 50, and I've kind of lost interest in writing books,'" Bob explains. "I still love writing copy, but if I don't write books, I want something else to do. My friend had been bugging me to do it, so without much thought, I put together my first product."

Bob was able to assemble his product in just a day or two. He owned the rights to a series of columns he had written for *Writer's Digest Magazine* on how to make six figures as a freelance writer. He added several more articles and other content he had written, gave it all to a graphic designer and ended up with an e-book called *Write and Grow Rich*.

It wasn't long before Bob was sold on internet marketing. "There's something about when you get the first check!" Bob exclaims. "That first sale on ClickBank or PayPal when you see, ding, $29 or $200 or whatever it is, it changes your life."

Bob has translated his experience into another product, "The Internet Marketing Retirement Program," to help others succeed. His program describes four stages of internet information marketing.

At his website, **Bly.com**, he has landing pages or domain names reserved for about 50 products. After only a year in the business, Bob already has 25 products and within a few months expects to have 50 or 60.

Bob is able to take his print books (to which he owns the copyrights), make simple updates and convert them into e-books. For example, a 200-page book turned into three e-books, and the increase in income derived from the electronic version was dramatic. "When I sold it originally, it was a $10 book. I would get 8 percent (80 cents). My agent would get his cut, so I'd end up with only 72 cents for that content. Now, it's three e-books priced at $29 or $39 each, so when I sell that same content, I get $90. Plus, I keep it all!" Bob says.

Now, Bob has gone from working 12-hour days to working less than 27 minutes a week on his info-business, and he's already making $200,000 a year. "I have a couple of assistants for my copywriting business, and I've given one of them some of the tasks of managing the online business. I outsource everything, so all I do is write my weekly e-mail," Bob explains.

His most recent e-mail for "The Internet Marketing Retirement Plan" has already netted 70 orders for his $100 product. To build on that success, Bob plans to do two things: create more products and send more e-mails.

"Developing more products is easy for me," Bob admits. "Having written so many books, I'm a content producer. I've discovered, though, that I'm very slow at learning some things: like the more you can e-mail to your list, the more money you'll make. Some people say you can't e-mail someone more than once a month. But we know that's nonsense."

Bob refers to Amy Africa, who runs a company called Eight by Eight: "Amy teaches internet marketing, and she says 98 percent of people out there don't mail often enough. They're leaving money on the table."

Bob has a monthly e-newsletter, and he e-mails to his list once or twice a week. "On Tuesday they get an e-mail about one of my products, and sometimes on Thursday we do a promotion for an affiliate," Bob says.

Bob uses a free reports squeeze page on his website to build his list. When customers visit **Bly.com/reports**, they can subscribe to his newsletter, *Bob Bly's Direct Response Letter.* When they subscribe, they get a marketing library—four of Bob's reports, worth over $100.

"So, we give them a big bribe," Bob laughs. "And then to build the subscriber list, we use a variety of means to drive traffic to the squeeze page."

Chapter 7

King Perseverance

Doubling Your Internet Sales Through Follow-Up

A S GOOD AS KING PRESENTATION AND KING CONSUMMATION ARE at what they do, they only succeed in bringing a few wanderers to the completion of their quests on the first attempt. The majority of visitors, even those who hear everything the kings have to say, leave the kingdom without doing anything.

The kingdom would not survive if it weren't for the efforts of King Perseverance, who follows those wanderers into the wilderness and convinces them to return to the kingdom.

To maximize your sales, you must follow the example of King Perseverance and follow up with everyone who opts in on your landing page. Follow-up can make the difference between a booming business and one that barely scrapes along.

To understand the importance of following up, you have to accept two basic facts.

First, you have to accept that most of your website visitors will click away without making a purchase on their first visit. You may convert 1 or 2 percent of your visitors right away, but even that is more than most businesses can hope for. The majority of internet merchants measure their conversion rates in fractions of 1 percent.

The second fact is that many of those visitors are still interested in your product or service, even though they didn't buy anything the first time around. People click away from your website for all sorts of reasons. They may not know exactly what they're looking for. They may want to look at your competitors. They may not have the money to make a purchase right away. They may have had to let someone else use the computer for a minute. They may have realized that they're missing a big game on TV. They may have stepped on their surge protector and turned off the computer by mistake.

And yes, some of them may simply have no interest in what you're selling. Still, you'd be crazy to let those uninterested visitors discourage you from following up with all those who might still turn into customers. Most of your visitors got to your website because they were looking for your type of product and service. If you play your cards right, you'll be able to get many of them back for a second visit.

How much difference does follow-up make? Take a look at Figure 7-1, which shows the number of sales generated by a client's website and the number of days that passed after each customer's initial visit.

The numbers speak for themselves. Twenty-one people made their purchases on the day of their first visit (that's day zero on the chart). Twenty-two made their purchases during the week that followed.

As you can see, most of the additional sales come in the first few days. Six customers made a purchase the day after their first visit, five of them came back to do it on the third day and so on. The numbers trail off a little bit each day, then spike back up to four on the last day because this campaign included a "last chance" offer in the seventh e-mail.

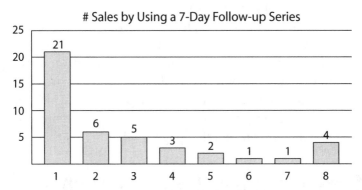

FIGURE 7-1. Notice how the number of sales doubles—at no cost—by using an autoresponder to send a series of follow-up e-mails.

What if this client hadn't used a follow-up campaign? He would still have those first-day sales, and maybe a few of his sales leads would have returned to make a purchase later without being prompted. At best, he'd be looking at 23 or 24 sales, compared to 43 with the follow-up campaign. Could you afford to leave that many sales on the table?

Brought to You by Your Landing Page

Your follow-up campaign is possible only because of your landing page. In the days before landing pages, businesses sent their visitors directly to a sales page or a homepage. They converted only a small percentage of those visitors into customers, and they had no idea who the other visitors were or what had happened to them. Today, by using a landing page as an intermediate step, businesses can collect information about their visitors and use that information to make sales after the fact.

This is a good thing for online stores, but it's even more important for businesses that use their websites to generate leads rather than to close sales. When you use your website to generate sales leads, you're planning to close sales in person, in print or over the phone. You have two options when it comes to doing that. You can take the passive approach, which means posting your phone number on a web page and hoping people will contact you after seeing your site. That's not likely to get you many sales. The active approach, in which you take the initiative to contact your sales leads after they visit your site, is the way to succeed, and your landing page is what makes that possible.

Your Secret Weapon: The Autoresponder

There are three ways to implement your follow-up campaign:

- Devote every waking hour to keeping track of your sales leads and sending each lead an e-mail every day.
- Hire a dozen extra employees to do the work.
- Use an autoresponder.

We're guessing you'll pick the third option, even if you're not sure what an autoresponder is.

An autoresponder, generally speaking, is any automated system that manages an e-mail list. It can be used to confirm orders, to reply to customer service questions and, most important, to send follow-up e-mails to your unconverted sales leads.

> Autoresponders are a must for information marketers on the internet. You can use the same one Bob Regnerus does by visiting **TheLeadsKingAuto Responder.com**.

Autoresponders aren't free, and the more sophisticated systems can cost several hundred dollars per month. Still, that's a drop in the bucket compared with the cost of sending your e-mails manually or losing sales by not sending them at all.

The Six Laws of King Perseverance

When planning your follow-up campaign, obey the six laws of King Perseverance. These laws will help you bring back as many unconverted sales leads as possible, and they'll help you avoid abusing the trust you've established with your sales leads.

Law #1: Timing Is Everything

The timing of your follow-up e-mails is sort of a high-wire act. On one hand, you want to bring your visitors back quickly because it becomes less likely that they'll become customers as time passes. On the other hand, you risk annoying your customers if you send too many e-mails in too short a time. Send more than one a day, and not only will you alienate your potential customers, you'll run the risk that they'll report you as a spammer.

We always fine-tune a follow-up campaign to fit the specific needs of a business or a client, but in general, we recommend sending a series of at least seven e-mails in the first two weeks after a visitor opts in. Sales trail off dramatically after those first two weeks go by, so that's your best opportunity to turn an unconverted lead into a customer.

That's not to say that you should give up on a potential customer after two weeks go by. It's less likely that a visitor will come back after that time, but it's not impossible. Many successful information marketers follow up with their sales leads for months, sending dozens of e-mails in the process. There's no additional work to sending those extra e-mails, so there's no reason to call it quits.

Law #2: Keep It Short

When your sales leads opted in on your landing page, they did it because they wanted to take advantage of your landing page offer and learn more about your products and services. They didn't necessarily realize they were also signing up to receive e-mails from you, even if you said so on the opt-in form. Don't give them an unpleasant surprise.

Your follow-up e-mails should be short and interesting. Keep them under 500 words, and say something new in each message. Use half your e-mails to talk about the general benefits of your product or service, and use the other half to discuss some of the finer points in detail. The last thing you want to do is alienate your potential customers by filling their inboxes with lengthy e-mails that repeat what you've already said in your sales presentation.

Law #3: Keep It Personal

When you use an autoresponder, you're writing e-mails that will be sent to a large number of people, and in most cases, you're typing up your entire sequence of follow-up e-mails at once. This tends to make your e-mails sound generic, so you have to make an effort to add a personal touch.

Any decent autoresponder will give you the ability to use your sales leads' names in your e-mails, so be sure to address everyone on your e-mail list by name. Don't start your e-mails with "Dear Valued Customer" or "To Whom It May Concern." You want to create the illusion that you typed up the e-mail a moment before you sent it.

The tone of your e-mails can help make them feel more personal. Aim for something midway between the casual tone of a blog post and the formality of a sales letter. You've "met" the people on your e-mail list before, when they visited your site, so you've already made your first impression. It's OK to relax a little bit when you contact them again.

Refer to the pages your leads visited on your website and to things you've said in previous e-mails. A sense of continuity and awareness will make your messages seem more personal.

Law #4: Ask Questions

Asking questions is one of the best ways to get your sales leads engaged. Use your e-mails to find out how people got to your website in the first place, whether they were happy with your landing page offer and what they thought of your sales presentation.

An even better use of your follow-up e-mails is to solicit questions from your sales leads. Encourage them to ask questions about your products or services or about the details of your offer. This will help you build a connection with your potential customers, and it will provide valuable information. If you find that your sales leads are all asking the same question, it means you have a hole in your sales materials.

Of course, if you solicit questions from your sales leads, you have to provide prompt answers. This isn't something your autoresponder can do for you, so make sure you have the resources to reply to all of your leads' questions the same day or next day.

Law #5: Include a Call to Action

Every follow-up e-mail must contain a new call to action. You're not sending these to entertain or educate—you want the people who get the e-mails to come back to your website and make a purchase.

Most of the time, you should ask your leads to go back for another look at your sales presentation. Your follow-up e-mails provide support to your sales materials, but if you're doing this right, you're not actually trying to close a sale with an e-mail. Send your leads back to your sales page, and let King Presentation do his job.

If you want to put in some extra effort, you can create a secondary sales presentation targeted specifically at your unconverted leads. Your follow-up presentation should contain less introductory material (your leads should know who you are and what you do by this point) and more detailed information about the benefits of your products or services. Providing fresh material, even if

For a free video on how to configure your auto-responder for maximum sales, visit **InternetInfo MarketingBook. com/autoresp.**

it's similar to your main sales presentation, is a good way to keep your leads interested.

Law #6: Use Offline Tools

Your follow-up campaign doesn't have to be limited to e-mail. Some autoresponders let you follow up with faxes, letters and even phone calls. You'll pay more for this type of service, but as with any type of sales support, if you do it right, it will pay for itself.

Sample Follow-Up Sequence

The sequence of sample e-mails below show you what a typical 10-day follow-up campaign might look like.

This is an actual series of e-mails Bob Regnerus uses to follow up with his sales leads. As you see, the e-mails are customized to address the recipient by name—these samples are intended for John Doe. The e-mails are short, conversational and benefit-focused, and each one contains a call to action.

Day 0

John - Your #1 Strategy for Getting New Business Online

Hello John,

Congratulations on wanting to grow your business using the internet. If you take these strategies and apply them, you will achieve the success you deserve by getting new clients in the door.

There's a huge void of practical, real-world advice for business owners on how to use the internet. Much of what you see taught is all moneymaking strategies for the internet, not the profit-producing information that real-world business owners need to grow an existing business using the internet.

So, let's grow your toolkit and your business at the same time!

First, let's focus on your website itself. (No use sending traffic to a website that's terrible at turning visitors into prospects.)

"If Your Website Is Nothing But a Brochure, You're Losing Potential New Clients and Wasting Your Traffic Driving Efforts"

I hate brochure websites. The only redeeming quality is that they look pretty. (You know, just like those popular girls and guys in high school, all looks, no substance!) These sites stink at selling. To me, if a website is good at selling, it's like a rose garden.

So, what kind of website sells?

A direct response website. One that requires the visitor to respond to a marketing message—a message directed to them personally and demands an action.

Look at your website. Is it pretty? Would it serve well as a brochure? Or does it sell?

When I do my infamous Traffic and Sales Maximizer Audit, www.TrafficandSalesMaximizerAudit.com, I typically find that the sites I review lack the fundamental elements of direct response, and therefore, do not sell.

I want to get you on the road to getting a website that sells.

Talk to you tomorrow about elements of a good direct response website …

Sincerely,

Bob Regnerus

Day 1

Hello John,

Yesterday I talked to you about direct response websites. Let's talk about an important concept you need to understand about your visitors.

"Web Visitors Are Easily Distracted"

You've got 7 seconds max once the visitor hits your page, so you better get to the point when they arrive. Don't waste space.

All of your important "online real estate" should be devoted to getting new business.

Make your website about the visitor, not you! BENEFITS. BENEFITS. BENEFITS.

Do this check on your site. Count how many times you use the words "I" and "we." If those outnumber the times you use the words "you" and "your," you have a website ego problem. Turn the flashlight around. Get it off your face and on to your prospect.

Also, pay attention to the "fold." (You know, like the fold of a newspaper?) What you see on the site first, without scrolling down or right, is considered "above the fold." You must use this space to get to the point. If you bury things below the fold or don't keep your prospect's attention, they have already clicked away.

One of the 21 elements I analyze in my Traffic and Sales Maximizer Audit (www.TrafficandSalesMaximizerAudit.com) is the fold. You'd be surprised how much I can help a client's landing page by putting certain elements "above the fold."

Talk to you tomorrow about some things to put above the fold ...

Sincerely,

Bob Regnerus

Day 2

Hello John,

We talked yesterday about making sure your important "online real estate" is devoted to getting new business.

To make your website about the visitor, not you, you need to state the benefits of your product or service. Reread that: benefits, NOT FEATURES!

Now about the "fold"... Here's one thing you absolutely need to have: A Headline.

What gets your attention in the newspaper, on TV or on the radio?

Headlines (or Teasers).

Tell me what you think is a better headline:

"Joe's Plumbing Service. Serving You Since 1983"

or

"We Guarantee That We'll Show Up at Your Door on Time, in a Clean, Pressed Uniform and Leave Your Home in Better Condition Than We Found It, or We'll Give You a $100 Bill."

Which headline is better?

Which plumber would you call?

Believe it or not, I see these "Since 19..." headlines all over the place in most business websites.

If you can't come up with something creative in your business, you don't deserve to be in business. Surely there's a reason you can create for people to do business with you.

It's called a USP or Unique Selling Proposition. Just putting this on your website will increase response, I guarantee it.

If you look at my site, www.FillMyFunnel.com, you'll notice I have a headline and copy that directs a message to the prospects I want to attract to my traffic management service. I am appealing to a business owner's sense of frustration about traffic and sales on their website.

Talk to you tomorrow about some more things to put above the fold …

Sincerely,

Bob Regnerus

Day 3

Hello John,

We talked yesterday about headlines—the big phrase or teaser that calls out to your prospects and alerts them to what you can do for them. With an effective headline, you've greatly increased the time a visitor will spend on your website.

Now that you have them there, you need to continue to speak to them and keep them there. You do that with compelling "copy" or content. First, they read your headline, and then they should start reading or listening or even watching your content and copy.

(For your benefit, think of copy being words that sell something and content being words that educate.)

Content and copy can be written words, spoken audio or even multisensory approaches using video. On a great website, you'll likely have all three, but most likely, you'll use words more than any other medium.

Just for an example, notice on FillMyFunnel.com how I use video to present my copy and then use words and video on my main site, www.TheLeadsKing.com.

Words are how we communicate, and words are still king, even on the internet. They're what the search engines "index," so it's important that you have good written content and copy on your website.

You need a balance of both on your website, and you need to know when the right time is to use them.

Look at your website. Read your website.

How's your content? Does it benefit the visitor? Are you using copy when it's time to sell? I hope so.

Talk to you tomorrow about some more things to put above the fold ...

Sincerely,

Bob Regnerus

Day 4

Hello John,

In discussing direct response websites so far, we've talked about headlines and compelling content and copy, especially above the fold.

This will ensure you call your prospect to attention, and keep his or her attention and convince him or her to stay on your website. (In the industry, this is called a "sticky" site.)

Sticky is a great visual term, isn't it? It's exactly what you want your site to do. A visitor becomes a prospect when he or she is captivated by your message and "sticks around."

The next thing you want to consider is your credibility. In a selling situation, you have a difficult job to do, and that's convincing someone that you are who you say you are, and you can do what you say you can do. It's also critical to prove that you've "done this before," and you can do it again and again.

This is done with testimonials, accreditations, images, proof of results, etc. Anything and everything you have to do to remove objections someone has about your ability and expertise.

Don't stop short on this, and don't skimp on this on your website. People are going to thoroughly check you out on your website before they contact you, so give the people what they want!

As an example, go to www.SalesMaximizerAudit.com. You will notice how I use video to make the site "sticky," and then within the video, I speak about those whom I've worked for, which shows my credibility.

On this site, we're offering a website design service, so I need to make sure prospects know that we've done this for clients in the past, and they were amazed at the results of our design.

To bolster this position, I also put testimonials below the video so people who scroll down can read about what I've done for clients.

Tomorrow, we'll get into the heart of the matter, the secret sauce that separates a brochure website from a website that sells.

Sincerely,

Bob Regnerus

Day 5

Hello John,

Headlines, content, copy, credibility. Everything you need to form a solid foundation for your website (if you care to make it an income-producing asset).

But that will do nothing for you if you forget the biggest thing: the "secret sauce" that separates websites that sell from websites that sit around and look pretty.

Think about the phrase "direct response."

Direct implies personal communication. In website terms, it's you speaking directly to your prospect through your website. Make it personal, using terms like "you" and "your."

Response means you, the marketer, *expect* a response from the prospect. No website can sell if you never allow for, or ask for, a response.

Reread that sentence. You expect and ask for a response. Simply put, you present a call to action.

All direct response websites have a call to action. And don't get confused when I say sell. You don't have to actually exchange service or product for money to be selling. Your call to action doesn't need to be an exchange of money, although it can be.

However, your call to action can be as simple as getting them to fill out a form or perhaps calling a phone number. So you don't need to be thinking "final sale." For most of you, this is the last thing you're thinking of.

As with most of my clients, they have a complex sales process, and most use the web to get prospects' mailing info, e-mail info or phone numbers.

Your call to action becomes a "sales job" to get them to take this action!

This involves careful planning and a process of determining objectives.

You've seen how I do this on my sites:

www.FillMyFunnel.com: Here I'm asking people to get my 4-CD set, "gratis."

www.SalesMaximizerWebsite.com: This is an offer for a quick-start evaluation on a website design. All I ask for is name, e-mail and number.

www.TheLeadsKing.com/quizpage: Here I offer a comprehensive marketing quiz and offer to send prospects their evaluations by e-mail.

So, you can offer a lot of things, but just remember, you need to make an offer!

Now that your website is in shape and has the ability to sell something, you're ready to go get some traffic! Traffic is the lifeblood of your website, and tomorrow we'll get into some hot ways to get traffic to your website to see your message!

Sincerely,

Bob Regnerus

Day 6

Hi John,

I fed you a lot in six days, didn't I? A great toolbox of ideas and strategies to prepare your website for visitors. Hopefully I've convinced you that brochure websites stink. I want you to have a website that sells because you'll get yourself an asset that produces income! Not one that depreciates over time.

Now, that's exciting!

But …

That asset needs fuel, needs blood, needs power. Here's how to do that.

Go get traffic, web traffic.

You've got to get people to your website; you can't wait for them to find you.

People think traffic is easy, but it's going to take a bit of effort. Some traffic is easier to get than others, but you need a plan, a strategy and a method for getting traffic to your site.

Over the next few days, I'll share some killer ways to get traffic, and if you master just these, you'll get enough traffic to get those clients you want. It's not all the traffic you can get, but certainly a place to start.

Today, let's start with the obvious. It's plastering your URL (website address) on everything that leaves your office.

In fact, I have a checklist of 50 more places to plaster your website address. If you send me a good online marketing question or a useful testimonial about what you've learned so far, I'll send you a copy.

Here's a start …

Flyers—Business cards—Yellow Pages ads—Your office sign—Your car—Your clothing

You get the idea. Wherever your prospects are hanging around, make sure they know where to find you on the web.

Tomorrow, I'll get into some pure web strategies for getting traffic to your website.

Sincerely,

Bob Regnerus

Day 7

Hi John,

We're talking traffic for the next few days. The lifeblood of your website is traffic, and I want to tell you how to get more of it!

Getting traffic to your website quickly is easy. *Very* easy.

Want to know how to get traffic to your website a couple of hours from now?

Warning—you have to pay for it, but if you know your numbers and you understand the concept of paying for advertising that results in profits, then this is something that you'll love.

It's called pay-per-click advertising, and it's my #1 strategy for my websites and my top clients.

There's nothing as quick and as targeted as pay-per-click advertising.

The concept is simple—you pay to place a small ad alongside search results on sites like Google.com, Yahoo.com and MSN.com when someone searches on "keywords" you pre-select.

For example, you are a home inspector. Therefore, you are pretty sure that when someone goes to Google to search for "home inspectors," they are probably looking to hire a home inspector.

You can set up an account at Google, write your ad and tell them you want to show your ad whenever someone searches on this term. You also have to tell them how much you're willing to pay when someone *clicks* on your ad and visits your website. Note that you pay when someone clicks, not when they see your ad. So you tell them you are willing to pay 50 cents, for example. If someone clicks on your ad 10 times, you are charged $5.

Now, I say it's easy, and I mean that, but only once you know what you're doing. You need to be careful when you start this. Make sure you understand the system because it's easy to run up your bill and eat up a lot of space on your credit card. I had it happen when I first started, and it's happened to clients before they came to me.

Once you know what you're doing, or work with an expert, you can start to see big returns on your investment.

Here's where you can get started with PPC advertising:

www.Google.com/adwords

http://SearchMarketing.Yahoo.com

http://Advertising.Microsoft.com/microsoft-adcenter

You *can* do this yourself, or you can hire someone to do it for you. We manage traffic for many clients, and if you want to learn about it, you can see a short presentation over at www.RoyalTrafficBuilder.com or get more strategies on my 4-CD set at www.FillMyFunnel.com.

Tomorrow, I'll talk about "artistic" ways of getting traffic to your site.

Sincerely,

Bob Regnerus

Day 8

Hi John,

Yesterday, you learned about a way to get listed on the first page of the major search engines. It's called pay-per-click advertising. Nothing gets you guaranteed qualified traffic so quickly and predictably.

Pay-per-click advertising is a science. It's all about the numbers. If you're able to work the numbers, PPC becomes a huge traffic source for your business, and you start to get the fuel to your site that gives it life and gets you the clients you want.

Today, I'm going to shift from science to art.

In PPC, you pay to be seen on the "right-hand side" of the search engine results, but you also want to be seen on the "left-hand side" of the results, known as natural or organic results.

This is also great traffic to get to your site because the people who find your website are very targeted, and the more words they use in their search phrase, the more targeted they become.

So ideally, as a home inspector in Chicago, you would love to be on page one of the organic results when someone types in "Chicago home inspector." You can be fairly confident that if someone is searching on this term, you have yourself a hot prospect if they click to your site.

This art is known as SEO (search engine optimization). It's the art of getting people to your website from the organic search engine results.

While SEO has some science to it, I call it an art because only the search engines know the "rules" or the algorithms they use to rank websites for a keyword phrase. There are large firms that study this and attempt to stay on top of the latest news, and people who do SEO for businesses with the hope of getting their clients ranked in the top 10 results for certain terms. (Top 10 results usually equals a page one listing and a lot of potential clicks.)

The best thing is, once you get these listings, the clicks are free. You aren't paying for them, so you want all you can get!

The problem is, this field is so ultra competitive and, in many markets, it's very difficult—nay impossible—to get ranked anywhere near page one.

It also usually takes an expert and a large investment to get many of your web pages ranked. It's manpower-intensive, and it takes three to six months to start seeing significant results.

Beware, there are a lot of scam artists and so-called experts in the SEO field. You need to be careful whom you listen to and careful whom you hire to do this for you.

We have a different approach for getting clients organic traffic. We're doing this for clients every day. You can read www.TheLeadsKing.com/client-success to hear from some of the clients we're promoting every day online.

If you want to read more about SEO, I suggest the following resources:

www.PlanetOcean.com

http://SearchEngineWatch.com

Tomorrow, I'll talk about some simple ways to gradually grow your traffic and make you a celebrity at the same time!

Sincerely,

Bob Regnerus

Day 9

Hi John,

PPC and SEO. Tired of strings of letters?

Me, too. Let's talk about something pretty cool today that will not only get you traffic, but will get you celebrity at the same time.

It's not really immediate, nor does it create floods of traffic all at once, but if you follow this method and do this on a regular basis, you'll start to see a huge upswing in traffic over time, and you'll start to see your name appear more and more on other websites and in the search engines.

It's called article marketing.

Articles are exactly what you think they are: 350–1,000 words of content that you create and distribute to directories and portals on the internet. These directories and portals are where big and small website publishers go to get content for their websites.

(Good content is hard to come by in many markets, and many site owners don't care to create content for themselves, so they go out and get it.)

So, if you or someone on your staff is an expert in one or more areas of the business, and it's something that people need to know about, you should get an article written.

For those of you who like to write, you can create the article yourself. Or you can hire a writer from a local college or one of the online free-lance sites. Another cool method is to record yourself talking, either alone or in an interview format. Then all you need to do is get it transcribed. Any of these methods works great—I've done them all.

Then you submit your site to various article directories, such as EzineArticles.com. This is one site where people go to get content for their own websites. The key is, you want to have a resource box at the end of your article that points back to your website so you get a back link, and you get your name out there.

What starts to happen after two to three months is that your article is suddenly appearing on hundreds, even thousands of websites all around the world. Your article is referring visitors to your website, or at least, you are getting links to your website (which is one of the key components of SEO optimization).

You'll start to gain popularity in the natural results, both on your articles and your own website because of all the incoming links. (This is one of the keys to doing SEO properly: getting links to your website.) You just need to be patient to let the other sites start picking up your content.

This sets you up in certain markets as a celebrity. If you've done some of this already, isn't it cool when you find your name or business listed on so many websites? If you just started SEO, then article marketing is a clever strategy to give yourself an SEO boost and get the organic traffic you want.

This is one of the most effective ways to get incoming links and to promote your website. I get into more details on this in my internet Success Blueprint CDs at www.FillMyFunnel.com.

Tomorrow, I'll talk about one more killer way to get a lot of traffic from offline and online sources.

Sincerely,

Bob Regnerus

Day 10

Hi John,

By now, you've received several strategies to get a lot of targeted traffic to your website. Some take work, some take a monetary investment.

I want to tell you about a cool traffic method that works like gangbusters if the strategy is used properly and it's timed and positioned correctly.

It's called PR, and you probably know about this type of marketing. PR is a great strategy for a business because you get an "official" endorsement at *no* charge by the media—TV, radio, newspaper, magazine, etc.

This strategy is used in many businesses, and they start this process by issuing press releases (PRs). Press releases are short, to-the-point announcements of events, promotions or news of interest to the public. Note that these articles must be of general interest to the public and not an ad. You need to write a press release differently from an ad, or even an article, because it has to capture the attention of the media editor and must have an angle that makes it newsworthy.

PR is something you don't do just one time; it must become an ongoing strategy so you start getting a good reputation with editors. Often you become a go-to person in an industry when news breaks. So, if you're a home inspector and there's a news event that talks about mold problems in local homes, the editor would have you on file and call you or interview you about how mold is a problem, how to detect it and how to eliminate it.

Once you start getting this type of publicity, there are all kinds of opportunities to leverage that in your business and use it for growth.

I like PR on the internet as well. Did you know there are websites that accept press releases and distribute them to online and offline media outlets?

One such service is PRweb.com. It's a service that will accept and publish your press releases. There's a free option, and it works OK, but their paid options for better promotion are probably a better deal.

This works, in effect, just like article marketing. You start to see websites posting these releases in their blogs. Local portals will pick these up and publish them in news feeds on their sites. Media outlets and "offline" publishers will pick these up when they need a source of news as well.

Depending on your timing and the newsworthiness of your release, you can certainly bring waves of traffic to your site when things line up properly. (Just make sure you clearly list your website in the release!)

I hope you've enjoyed these series of messages. I know I didn't have the time and space in these short messages to put a lot of explanation behind these strategies.

I put up a lot of information in my blog on a regular basis at www.TheLeadsKing.com/blog.

Are you ready to start growing your business using the internet? At last, you now have someone who lays it all out for you and gives you the exact plan you need to make your website sell, making it a true income-producing asset for your business.

You owe it to yourself to get my Internet Success Blueprint CDs at www.FillMyFunnel.com.

Sincerely,

Bob Regnerus

Info Marketer Profile

As the "E-Zine Queen," Alexandria Brown Rules

Seven years ago, Alexandria Brown was an account manager and copywriter for a small ad agency in New York City. Today she is the "E-zine Queen," and she likes—no, loves—being in charge of her own destiny.

Alexandria thinks back to her New York days: "I knew I wanted to work for myself because I had moved from job to job looking for *the* job that would make me happy. I finally realized I just wanted to be on my own."

Hers is a familiar story. Old-fashioned bosses. Bureaucracy. Management by committee. "I had better ideas than my bosses did, and they wouldn't let me make any changes. I like to make changes fast," Alexandria laughs. "It took them five months to decide what new fax machine to buy. It was just driving me crazy, and I started thinking: I could go to Staples today, buy everything I need and have clients by next week. So I left ... but I was in for a rude awakening. I didn't realize how important marketing is ... For a while there, I starved!"

Alexandria did everything you're supposed to do. She studied marketing. She went to networking meetings. "But it just wasn't clicking for me," Alexandria says. "Finally, I tried an e-mail newsletter to promote my services to people I'd already met. I started with 10 people, which included my parents and my cat," she laughs. "I didn't have a website, products to sell or anything."

She started out by sharing a marketing tip of the week. Soon, people started forwarding Alexandria's e-mails, and her list started to grow. Within a few months, Alexandria had gotten some referrals to big clients like D&B, *New York Times Digital* and Scholastic Books. "I wasn't selling my information yet, but the information was definitely marketing for me," she says.

➡

At the beginning of her information marketing career, Alexandria took a straightforward, no-nonsense approach to her e-mail newsletter. "Up until three or four years ago, I didn't feel I should share anything personal in the newsletter," Alexandria says. "I had moved to California, and all this stuff was going on in my life, relationships and things, but I didn't share anything. I just talked about marketing."

All that changed when Alexandria got a new kitten.

"I already had two other cats—and was delighted to get a new one—but at the same time, I had forgotten how crazy kittens are," Alexandria laughs. "This kitten was bipolar, sweet and sleeping one minute and the next running around like Tom and Jerry. The cats were all chasing each other around the house, knocking things over, going up the drapes, across my desk, jumping on my head, and there I was trying to write the newsletter! I was getting aggravated, so I started writing just a little bit about the kitten, saying, 'Oh, you know, it's funny. I'm trying to get this newsletter out today, but this kitten is driving us all crazy. She's so cute, but what a handful.' That was it. Really just a sentence or two. I had this great article underneath it on how to write headlines, and I'm thinking, 'They're going to love this article. This is going to rock their world.'"

Alexandria pressed "Send," and the response rocked *her* world.

"I went out for the day," Alexandria recalls. "I came back and had dozens and dozens of e-mails about the cats. The cats! They cared about the cats. People were writing me back saying, 'What are your cats' names? How many cats do you have? How long have you had the cat? What kind of kitten is it? Can you show us pictures?' People were sending me pictures of their cats. Some of them were dressed up. It's kind of freaky. This one woman wrote and said, 'Now that I know you love cats, I'm going to buy everything you have.' And I still see her name on my customer list," Alexandria marvels.

With those few lines about her cats, Alexandria discovered that great marketing—whether in person, in print or online—is all about making a connection. "When it comes to online marketing, we think it's different, but actually it's even more important that you build a relationship with your online readers," she says.

Now, Alexandria makes it a habit to share information with her customers about what's going on in her life. She includes a few personal notes in her e-zine, and she uses her blog (**AlexandriaBrown. blogspot.com**) to post photos and write more about herself. This creates a strong connection with her list. "Some people tell me outright, 'I didn't even read your article, but I wanted to hear about your vacation and your first time waterskiing,'" Alexandria says. "I like having the blog because if anyone wants to see photos or read more about my life, they can go there. It's amazing that when you're a little bit vulnerable with customers and you share what's going on in your life, they will respond to that. People buy from people they know, like and trust."

Alexandria built on the success of her e-zines by publishing an e-book on how to use e-zines to market products and services. "Within a year or two, I had people saying, 'Hey, Ali, you're not at these networking meetings anymore, and we see you wearing nicer suits, and you're obviously getting better clients, and everything's going great for you. What is the secret?' I said, 'Well, you gotta start one of these e-zines,' and they said, 'How do we do it?'" Alexandria recalls.

So, she looked in the bookstores, and she looked online. "I was not really happy with any of the books or courses I found on e-zines, so I decided to write one. At first, I was going to write a 'real' book until I realized that it's time-consuming and you don't make much money on printed books," Alexandria says.

➡

Alexandria put together her first e-book and sent a quick e-mail to her list. "That was the moment my life changed!" she exclaims. "By that time, I had amassed a few thousand people on my list—my 'herd' as Dan Kennedy calls it—but I didn't know the power of what I was doing. I started my e-zine to get more clients, and when I came out with this e-book, I thought maybe my clients would be interested in it. So, I put up a crappy website and wrote a note to my e-mail list saying, 'Hey, you may be interested in this. It's a course on how to publish an e-zine that makes you sales and clients and makes you more money.' I remember pressing 'Send,' and then the sales just came in.

"That was the day my life just completely changed because I had shifted from selling my *time* to selling my *knowledge*. I suddenly had leverage. I suddenly realized the amount of money I could make was no longer linked to the amount of hours I worked. I was done with that book, and the sales kept coming in and coming in and coming in. And to this day, it still makes me money. I have a much more advanced version of it now, but it's essentially based on the same information."

Over time, Alexandria was able to cut back on the number of clients she served and spend more time on her own continuing education and her information marketing business. Not everyone understood this shift in her focus, let alone her new e-book business.

"My friends and family were like 'What are you doing?!' They did not understand," Alexandria laughs. "My mom even said, 'No one's going to buy a book that's not even real for $29!'"

It turns out lots of people were willing to pay $29 (and lots more!) for a book "that's not even real." Last year, Alexandria's business grossed $1.1 million. But to be completely fair to Alexandria's mom, many people do still want a "real" book. Along with the ➡

success of the e-book came requests for it in printed form. "I actually do a lot more physical products now than digital," Alexandria says. "We have found there's a lower return rate, and people stick with it longer. They actually use the product better."

Alexandria uses a combination of marketing strategies to promote her products, including article writing, public speaking and tele-seminars, but her focus is always the same: "The *who* is more important than the *what*," she says. "Where is your target market already? Where are they hanging out? Who has access to them in large numbers?"

While she focuses on strategies that connect her to people within her target market, she is also getting started with paying someone to do lead generation via SEO and Google AdWords, and e-mail forwards continue to help build her list.

One of her best target markets are coaches, and Alexandria has found associations and other organizations that count thousands of coaches among their members. She approaches these groups and offers a free tele-seminar or an article for their newsletters. "At the very least, I'll pay to advertise," she says. "The key is to be in front of them. It's locating those centers of influence in the market you want to reach that can really speed up the process."

Alexandria's current business is fairly evenly divided among three revenue streams: products, live events and coaching.

Alexandria has expanded on her e-zine and e-book business to include printed manuals and kits. Her bestselling "Boost Business With Your Own E-zine" currently sells for $497, and her "Online Success Blueprint in a Box" currently sells for $1,497. "I've come a long way from the $29 e-book," she says with a smile. "And I'm adding another new product called 'Workshop Marketing Secrets' that walks people step-by-step through my plan for marketing a workshop or seminar."

Alexandria comments about the thing she never thought she would do—coaching:"I didn't think I wanted to deal with people, but I realized that what people want most is someone to connect with. So, I set up programs and ways that don't take a lot of my time, but still give people access to me," Alexandria says.

Most of her coaching programs involve group calls. Only her platinum clients have one-on-one calls with Alexandria. These elite members get six 15-minute emergency calls per year."I use the word *emergency*, and it's amazing when you use that word—they really save those calls for something important," Alexandria chuckles.

Her gold and silver members participate in group calls, and by using bridge line technology and tele-seminars, Alexandria can coach hundreds of people at a time. She also provides CDs and transcripts of the calls, and hosts an online forum where members can interact with each other.

Live events make up another third of Alexandria's business. As with everything else she does, good marketing is the key to success."When people are going to spend several thousand dollars on an event, you have to answer a lot of questions they have in their minds," Alexandria says."An informational page alone does not do the work. So, at a bare minimum, I do at least one free tele-seminar that I know answers a lot of their questions." She also makes sure she answers every objection she can think of in her sales letter."I tell people when they're writing a sales letter for their event to go through all the common objections they think their target market might have as an excuse not to attend. For example, 'It's too far to travel' or 'It's too much money' or 'I think I know this stuff already.' Any of those things you have to address in the sales letter," Alexandria explains.

She has found that no one wants to be the first person to attend a seminar. "You have to use testimonials, what some people call 'social proof,'" she says. During her free tele-seminars, she has several past clients who have dramatically increased their business with what they have learned from her get on the phone. "They just rave about me. I don't have to say anything," Alexandria marvels. "Success stories really speak for themselves."

Indeed. Alexandria runs her business from a beautiful new beach house in Los Angeles, working only four days a week. "I'm happy to keep a business with smaller numbers, but with a higher value. I'm always looking for ways to work less to make the same money or even more," she says. "The big selling point for the information marketing industry is the lifestyle. I'm a big vacation person. I love going away—a lot. It also makes me feel really good that I can get on a plane anytime and go visit my elderly parents. I don't have to ask anyone for permission, and I can work from wherever I am if I want to."

Part of Alexandria's freedom stems from the way she has chosen to run her business. She uses a virtual team of five stay-at-home moms who play different roles in Alexandria's operation. "I have no one working with me in my home. I don't necessarily want to get dressed every morning. I don't want to see anybody in the morning. I don't want to talk to anybody in the morning," Alexandria chuckles. "It's very valuable for people to get clear on what they want their lives to look like. I almost did the office thing, and I'm so glad I didn't!"

Alexandria offers some advice for others who also might not want to do "the office thing":

"If you already have an area of expertise, go with that," Alexandria says. "I've had clients come to me, for example, and they are brilliant tax accountants, but they want to start an information marketing business on poodle grooming because they love poodles. I'll say, 'You know what? That's great, but why don't we look at where you already have credibility and expertise?'

"If you're an expert in tax accounting, why not write a book or an audio program on '29 Ways to Pay Less Taxes in Your Small Business?' You should start with an area you are very strong in, and the very first step you should take—and this is where most people make a big mistake—the very first step you should take is to build your herd," Alexandria stresses. "Most folks start by creating a product. They get all excited about the product and everything it does and offers and how great it is. And they get stuck there. This still happens even in my advanced coaching groups like my platinum group. I have to really drill it into their heads—creating another product is not going to solve their marketing problems!"

Building a list is fairly straightforward, according to Alexandria. "Most small business owners are already out there promoting their businesses. What they should be doing is collecting people's names and e-mails and mailing addresses."

She offers these examples: "When you're speaking at an event, if the promoter will let you do it, offer a free drawing for your product or even just a coffee mug. People go nuts to win something on stage, and then you collect hundreds of business cards at one time. I also tell them they'll receive a complimentary subscription to my award-winning e-zine *Straight Shooter Marketing*. If you exhibit at trade shows, you can conduct drawings to collect business cards. It's that simple. If you're already out and about in marketing or business, make it your priority to build your list."

Alexandria also uses articles she has written to market herself. "You know, most people just let articles die after they write them. But there are a hundred different ways you can use those articles. You can get them inserted in publications that your target market reads. Plus, there are websites all over the internet where you can post content that other authors or other publishers will pick up and use."

Chapter 8

King Enticement

The Secret to Getting More Customers Is Not More Traffic

THE SECRET TO GETTING MORE CUSTOMERS IS MORE *TARGETED* traffic. King Enticement must send the right type of visitor to his kingdom, or it won't matter how well King Salutation, King Presentation, King Consummation and King Perseverance do their jobs. The visitor will never complete his or her quest, and the kingdom will gain nothing from the kings' efforts.

Driving thousands of people to your website will do you no good if those people aren't likely to buy what you're selling. The trick is to attract people who are actively looking for your type of product or service and who are motivated to make a purchase.

Right Traffic vs. Wrong Traffic

When I (Bob Regnerus) start working with a new client, my team and I use a tool we call the Traffic and Sales Maximizer Audit to evaluate the client's existing website and marketing campaign. The audit includes a 21-point assessment of the client's landing page, and that's often where we find problems. Most landing pages are missing key elements like a strong headline or call to action, and they're often cluttered with unnecessary text.

Some clients, however, are doing all the right things on their landing pages, but their conversion rates are still lower than they should be. When I see that, I know right away what the problem is: The website is not getting targeted traffic.

A website that isn't getting targeted traffic actually has two problems. It's not getting enough of the right traffic, and it's getting too much of the wrong traffic.

Many business owners have trouble grasping the concept of "the wrong traffic" because they think more is always better. This is definitely not the case. If you were running a shoe store, would you want to fill the aisles with people looking for ball gowns, fruit juice and motor oil? Of course not! They'd prevent your real customers from trying on shoes, and they'd waste your time asking useless questions.

Visitors who come to your website but have no intention of buying anything can cause the same kinds of problems. Just by coming to your site, they can slow the site's performance and force you to spend money on additional bandwidth. Some of them may opt in without paying attention to your landing page copy, which means you'll lose time following up with them later or responding to questions that have nothing to do with your business. An effective traffic campaign attracts the right visitors and tells the wrong ones to look elsewhere.

In this chapter, you learn how to drive targeted traffic to your site. When you follow these guidelines, you convert more visitors to customers, and you spend less time on lost-cause sales leads.

A Few Words About Keywords

Before you start driving traffic to your site, you need to understand keywords.

"Keywords," to put it simply, are the words you want associated with your website. They're the words you think your customers will use when they do internet searches for your type of product or service. No matter how you drive traffic to your site, you need to start with a good keyword list.

Good keyword lists are not small—we're usually not happy with a list until it includes more than 1,000 words. That sounds like a lot of work, but there are lots of tools that can help you build your list, and you don't have to do it all at once. You can get a good start in a few hours, and if you know where to look, you'll be able to refine and improve your list as you move forward with your campaign. Here are some of the resources you can use to find your keywords:

Your head: This is your single best source of keyword ideas. Before you look for keywords anywhere else, sit down at your computer or grab a pad of paper and put yourself in your customers' shoes. If you wanted to buy your own product or service, what keywords would you use to search for it? Those are the words you should start with.

Sales materials: You can get keyword ideas from your product descriptions, manuals, sales presentations and other materials, whether they're on your website or not. Look for the words or phrases you use to identify your company or products, and look for words that differentiate you and your company from your competitors.

Customers: Ask your customers how they found you—find out which websites they used for their searches and which words they searched for.

Website stats: You need to know which words your visitors are searching for before they come to your site, so read your web traffic reports or have your web administrator do it for you. You'll see that you're getting traffic from some of the words you came up with on your own, but you'll also get new words and new ideas. Once your site has been up for a few months, you'll have plenty of data to work with.

Google Analytics: Google Analytics is a great tool for website owners. It provides dozens of reports that tell you how people found your site, what they did while they were there and where they went when they left. There's no fee to use the service, and you can set it up in a matter of minutes. See Chapter 9 for more about Google Analytics.

Keyword services: When you need extra help with your keyword list, you can use tools specifically designed for keyword research. These keyword services are enormous databases of internet search statistics and trends. Keyword services have access to more information than you could ever look through yourself, so they can help you come up with keywords that might be less common but will still be effective for you.

Google's AdWords system has a useful keyword service, which is available for free to anyone with an AdWords account. When you enter one of your existing keywords, the tool returns a list of related keywords that Google users have searched for, along with a rough estimate of each word's search volume.

Keyword tools are not all alike. Bob Regnerus recommends this one for most information marketers: **TheLeadsKingKeyword Software.com.**

If you need to dig deeper, subscription services such as Wordtracker and Keyword Discovery can give you more personalized results. You'll pay about $50 a month for the service, but if you're in a highly competitive or highly specialized market, it's probably worth the money.

Quality Matters

No matter where you find your keywords, it's important to look for quality. There's an 80/20 rule to keyword research: 80 percent of your website traffic will come from 20 percent of your keywords.

Adding hundreds and hundreds of random words to your list isn't likely to increase your traffic, so put your effort into finding *better* keywords rather than *more* keywords.

Paid Traffic vs. Organic Traffic

You have two options when you want to generate traffic for your website: You can pay for it, or you can generate it organically. To put it in general terms, paid traffic comes from advertising; organic traffic comes from word-of-mouth.

Paid Traffic

Eventually, you'll want to drive traffic using both paid and organic methods, but if you're starting out, it's best to start by paying for your traffic. Paid traffic starts flowing more quickly than organic traffic, and it's easier to track.

That second point is important—always pay close attention to the performance of your traffic campaign, or you'll miss sales opportunities and waste money.

The most common (and important) method of buying traffic is pay-per-click advertising. We talk about pay-per-click in detail, and we take a look at the other common sources of paid traffic, such as banner advertising and affiliate programs.

Focus on using pay-per-click for the first few months, but in the long term, plan to add as many types of paid traffic as you can manage. Things change all the time in the world of internet marketing, so if you rely on one source for your traffic, your sales could really take a hit with the next advance in technology or shift in consumer behavior.

Pay-per-Click Advertising

"Pay-per-click" advertising is exactly what it sounds like: a system in which you pay a fee every time someone gets to your website by clicking on an ad.

This is where you put your keyword list to work. When you open a pay-per-click account with Google AdWords or another system, you supply your list of keywords and ask the service to display your ad when someone uses one of your keywords in an internet search. You also tell the service how much you're willing to pay when someone clicks on your ad. The more you're willing to pay, the more likely your ad will be shown.

Several factors determine where and when your ad gets displayed. Most pay-per-click services use an auction system for their ads, so if you enter a low bid on a common keyword, you won't get any results. You may need to pay several dollars for the most popular keywords in your market.

Money isn't the only factor, though. Google and some of the other services look at the quality of your ads. The quality of an ad is determined by how closely it relates to a given keyword and how often people respond to the ad by clicking on it. If your ads are good enough, you can win good placement for your ads even if you're not the highest bidder.

An understanding of pay-per-click advertising, especially the Google AdWords system, is essential to the success of your information marketing campaign. Let's take a detailed look at how pay-per-click works, starting with the 800-pound gorilla.

Google AdWords

The next time you do a search on Google, take a close look at the search results page. You'll see three distinct sets of results.

In the larger column, on the left side of the screen, are the organic results. Those are based on Google's index of websites, and they're ranked in order of relevance to your search. We come back to the organic results later in this chapter.

Over on the right side of the screen, under the "Sponsored Links" heading, is a vertical column of pay-per-click ads. In the shaded box above the organic results, you see another set of pay-per-click ads. This group of ads is placed by Google AdWords, the largest advertising system on the internet, and the main reason Google raked in over $16 billion in 2007.

The ultimate goal of your pay-per-click campaign is to win placement for your advertisements at the top of that "Sponsored Links" column, or if you really play your cards right, in that shaded box above the organic results.

Your traffic-generating campaign should start with Google AdWords, for a number of reasons:

Google is the largest search engine in the world, and AdWords is the largest pay-per-click service. This means that AdWords gives you access to more potential customers than any other service.

It takes very little time to set up an AdWords campaign. You can open an account in about 20 minutes, and your ad can be up and running in less than one day. AdWords provides excellent instructions and help features, and it's the easiest system to use, from the advertiser's point of view.

AdWords ads are attractive to users because they don't really look like ads. They're plain text in three colors, so visually there's not much to separate them from the organic search results.

Google has a large content network. The Google Network is made up of other websites (like **About.com** and **HowStuffWorks.com**) that display AdWords ads on their pages. You have the option to display ads on Google only or on sites in the content network as well.

Google provides Google Analytics, the best free reporting package you'll ever find.

Again, as your marketing campaign evolves, you'll want to add traffic sources in addition to AdWords. When you're new to pay-per-click advertising, though, no other system provides nearly as much value or support.

Opening Your AdWords Account

To open a pay-per-click account with Google AdWords, go to **AdWords.Google.com** and click the link to "Sign up now." The system walks you through a five-step process:

1. Choose an edition: If you're doing this on your own, choose the Starter Edition, which streamlines the entire process. You can switch to the Standard Edition once you get the hang of the system. Make sure to tell Google that you already have a website.

2. Targeting options: This is where you choose the language and geographical region in which you want your ad displayed.

3. Write your ad: Next, write your ad. You get 25 characters for your headline and two 35-character lines of text. This is also the step where you provide the link to your landing page.

Notice that you have a lot more room for the "Destination URL" than for the "Display URL." This feature allows you to test the effectiveness of different landing pages while using the same ad copy— remember not to test too many different things at once.

4. Choose your keywords: Submit the keywords from your list, and use Google's keyword tool to look for keywords you might have missed.

5. Account setup: In the last few steps of the process, provide your target budget and contact info. Once you get an e-mail from Google and confirm your billing information, your ad starts running.

After you've set up your account, the next step is to go into your campaign settings and adjust your keyword bids. By default, Google sets all your keyword bids to the same maximum cost-per-click, but you'll want to bid higher on certain words and lower on others.

Generally speaking, we advise clients to take an aggressive strategy and bid high on their most important keywords. At the beginning, though, you're better off setting a low monthly budget and bidding low on your keywords. This gives you time to learn the ins and outs of the system and measure the performance of your keywords without breaking the bank.

The Google Quality Score

Your keyword bids are the most important factor in determining where and when your ads appear, but your "Quality Score" plays an important part as well.

You're assigned a different Quality Score for each of your keywords, and AdWords looks at that score each time someone searches for one of your keywords. Your Quality Score is based on several factors, including the content of your landing page and your click-through rate—that's the percentage of people who click on your ad after seeing it.

Google won't say exactly what it looks at when it evaluates landing pages, and it won't tell you exactly what your Quality Score is. That makes it more difficult to improve your score, but you have to work at improving it, or your campaign won't reach its potential. This is especially important at the beginning of your campaign. Google treats new advertisers with suspicion, so you have to prove that you can write a decent ad, follow the rules for bidding and keep people on your site once they click on your ad.

To improve your quality score, track your ads' performance and rewrite those that aren't generating clicks. If you have more than one campaign running at a time, don't let one fall by the wayside—Google looks at the performance of every ad you run, even if it's part of a different campaign. Also, be sure to follow the rules for "Optimizing

Your Landing Page for Google" in Chapter 4. You have to appeal to Google as well as to your sales prospects.

Yahoo! Search Management and Microsoft AdCenter

Once you have your Google AdWords campaign up and running, it's time to expand your efforts to the other two major pay-per-click systems. Yahoo! Search Management and Microsoft AdCenter aren't as big or easy to use as AdWords, but they both get a lot of search traffic, so it's best not to ignore them. In some cases, the Yahoo! or Microsoft systems perform better than AdWords, usually at a lower cost.

There's another reason to run campaigns with several systems at once—you protect yourself in the event that AdWords makes drastic changes to the way it assigns ad space. That's happened before, and we've seen careless marketers lose 90 percent or more of their traffic overnight as a result.

Setting up your accounts with Yahoo! and Microsoft is a little more time-consuming than setting up an AdWords account, but you won't need to do nearly as much work to develop or test your campaigns because you've already done that work on AdWords. Tweak your ads and keyword lists, if necessary, and then start running them on the other systems. Whenever you learn something new from your AdWords reports or Google Analytics, be sure to apply the knowledge to your other pay-per-click campaigns.

Other Sources of Paid Traffic

Just as you should advertise with more than one pay-per-click service, you should use other sources of traffic in addition to pay-per-click. For one thing, pay-per-click won't reach every potential customer, and for another, it's usually the most expensive source of traffic. The other methods of paying for traffic don't produce the same results as pay-per-click, but if you use them wisely, they justify the investment.

Banner advertising. Anyone who has ever used the internet knows what a banner ad looks like—it's a colorful, sometimes animated advertisement along the top or side of a web page. These miniature billboards used to be popular. They were actually Yahoo!'s main source of revenue for years, but they're no longer a primary source of traffic for most websites. Banner ads lost most of their appeal once internet users got used to them and learned to ignore them. They tend to annoy users now, and many browsers and security programs include banner-ad blocking functions.

Still, banner advertising is alive and kicking, and even Google AdWords offers a banner advertising option for its content network (you won't get a banner ad on Google itself, though).

Affiliate programs. We've mentioned affiliate programs several times in this book. You can make extra money by acting as an affiliate for other websites, and you can also drive traffic to your website by starting your own affiliate program. In the long run, you get more benefit from hiring affiliates than from being one yourself.

For most information marketers, starting an affiliate program from scratch is a little too much work. You'll probably want to use a service like Infusion Software (**TheLeads KingCRM.com**) to manage your program for you.

Infusion Software contains a powerful and easy-to-manage affiliate management application: **TheLeadsKingCRM.com**.

Sponsorships. You can generate extra traffic by sponsoring websites your potential customers are likely to visit. Many nonprofit organizations refuse to accept normal advertising, but will accept "sponsorships." To understand the difference between the two, think of the differences between network TV ads and the sponsor announcements you see on PBS.

Usually these sites allow you to describe your business, but they won't let you make statements directed toward their visitors. You'll get some traffic from the sites you sponsor, and if you include their logos on your own site, you'll also help boost your credibility.

Offline advertising. Radio, print and TV advertising can be effective in driving traffic to your website. You can either develop new campaigns specifically for this purpose or add your web address to your existing ads.

The same strategy applies to offline and online advertising—whenever possible, provide the specific address of your landing page rather than your home page. King Salutation is always the best man for the job of greeting visitors, no matter how they get to your website.

Paid directories. Many websites offer to list your website in a directory in exchange for a fee. Some of these websites charge a fee for every listing, but the more important ones, including Google's Local Business Center and Yahoo! Local, offer two options. You can get a free listing by entering your information, or you can pay for a more prominent listing. We take a closer look at these sites later in the chapter, in the section on local business directories.

Organic Traffic

"Organic traffic" is the alternative to paid traffic, but it's not the same as *free* traffic. When you drive organic traffic to your site, you still pay for it, but you pay for it with time and effort instead of money. Don't think of it as a shortcut or as a replacement for paid traffic. Once you have the hang of pay-per-click and the other paid traffic sources, this is the next step in your traffic-generating campaign.

There are four ways to generate organic web traffic:

- Search engine optimization
- Website promotion
- Local business directory listings
- In-house traffic generation

We look at each of these traffic sources, starting with the most important: search engine optimization.

Search Engine Optimization

While you can pay to improve the visibility of your pay-per-click advertisements, you don't have the same option when it comes to your placement in organic search engine results. Most reputable search engines, including the big three (Google, Yahoo! and Microsoft), do not accept payment in return for higher placement in their search results.

That doesn't mean you can't improve your standing in organic results. There are several things you can do to get your website listed higher. Some of those tools and methods will support your other marketing efforts, and others can get you into trouble. The general name for trying to improve a website's search engine ranking is "search engine optimization," SEO for short.

SEO rules change week by week and month by month because search engines constantly change the way they rank websites in their listings.

No search engine will disclose its exact ranking method, but in every case the process starts with a program called a "spider." Spiders crawl through the internet day and night, reading websites, exploring links, looking for changes. Every search engine builds an index of the websites their spiders have read and then analyzes the index to determine which pages will be most useful to the search engine's users.

Search engine placement can make or break an online business, so an entire industry has grown up around improving search engine results. SEO specialists describe their work in three ways:

"White hat" SEO means increasing the readability, quality and relevance of a website. Visitors to white hat sites have a good chance of finding what they're looking for.

"Black hat" SEO means creating a useless site or manipulating an irrelevant site to artificially inflate its ranking and attract traffic. Visitors who come to black hat sites usually click back to the search results page immediately.

"Gray hat" SEO means using black hat methods to improve the ranking of a relevant site. Visitors to gray hat sites should be as happy with the result as visitors to white hat sites.

Whether you're doing your SEO on your own or hiring someone to do it for you, you'll need to understand the basic concepts behind each type.

White Hat SEO

When you use white hat SEO, you're playing by the rules. You're adding content that your visitors will want to read, and you're representing your site accurately to the search engines. Visitors to your site find what they expect to find, so they don't immediately click back to the search results page.

Search engines want to reward sites that play by the rules, so even when the ranking systems change, these fundamental qualities maintain their importance. If you include the elements below, you should not ever have to worry about a sudden drop in your search engine ranking.

Good content. Search engines reward websites for providing original content—content that can't be found on any other site. They also look for content that's updated regularly and includes multimedia elements such as video and audio. In general, what's interesting to a human visitor will be interesting to a search engine.

It's important that your keywords appear frequently in your website's content, but you have to walk a thin line between omitting keywords and using them too often. Repeating words over and over makes your site less interesting to your visitors, and it makes search engines suspicious.

Site maps. Many websites have started using drop-down or pop-up menus rather than traditional links to lead visitors through the site. Those menus are nice-looking, and they often make things easier for visitors, but they cause big problems for search engines.

The problems arise because search engine spiders don't have the tools to move through sites that use Flash or Java programming—that's what you're using when you have drop-down or pop-up menus. When a spider can't read a page, the page doesn't get indexed, so it won't show up in the engine's search results.

This doesn't mean that drop-down menus are bad or that you shouldn't use them. It means you have to provide normal links to all of your pages as well so search engines can access all the content on your site. The best way to do this is by providing a site map, which is basically a table of contents for your website with a link to each page on the site.

Accurate titles and metadata. Search engines look at the descriptive information hidden in your website's programming, such as the page titles, tags and metadata. Your web programmer, if you use one, should know all about these elements. If you build your website on your own, be careful with your titles and metadata.

A web page's title is the word or phrase that appears in the title bar at the top of the visitor's browser window. Many search engines pay extra attention to page titles, so make sure yours are descriptive and accurate.

Metadata provides additional information about the content on a web page. Early black hat techniques focused on metadata, so search engines learned to assign less importance to it. Even though it's less important now, some search engines still look at metadata, so include a few relevant meta items in your programming.

Reciprocal links. Google became the world's leading search engine almost overnight. One of the main reasons for Google's success was that it was the first engine to look at links on other websites when determining the importance of a web page. The more pages that link to a website, the more relevant Google believes it will be to its users.

Every search engine looks at external links now, so when you begin your SEO campaign, try to convince other website owners to link to your site. The easiest way of doing this is to offer reciprocal links to the websites that link to yours.

This is something you need to be careful about, though. If you set up reciprocal linking arrangements with websites that have nothing in common with your own, search engines punish you rather than reward you.

Try to get links on pages your visitors will be interested in and that have content similar to your own. The more popular a website is, the harder you should try to set up a linking arrangement with its owners. Search engines consider importance of the pages that link to yours, in addition to the total number of pages.

Frequent updates. Search engine spiders recognize when a web page has new content, and the more often they find new content, the more often they come back for another look. This improves your ranking because search engines assume that their visitors will be more interested in fresh content.

This is one of the many reasons you should add a blog to your website—it's the fastest and easiest way to add content to your site.

Black Hat SEO

Since even the most secretive search engines eventually provide clues about their ranking systems, black hat SEO specialists can find ways to manipulate the system and artificially improve their clients' rankings.

These days, black hat SEO usually isn't worth the effort because search engines have the advantage. They have more people (and smarter people, for the most part) working for them, so they're able to stay ahead of the SEO game. Each time a search engine makes a change in its ranking algorithm, the SEO specialists have to start over.

What does this means to you? It means that if you hire someone to do black hat SEO, you'll never be off the hook. Whenever Google or the others refine their rankings, you'll have to get out your wallet and pay for another round of black hat tricks.

There's another, equally important reason to avoid black hat SEO: blacklisting. Search engines have a strong interest in discouraging SEO tricks, so when they discover a website using black hat SEO, they remove the site from their results and add it to a list of sites ineligible for indexing. It can be difficult or impossible to get off a blacklist, so don't put yourself in a position where that can happen to you.

Even though we don't recommend using them, we're going to describe the most common black hat SEO techniques here, for two reasons. First, you should know what they are and why they don't work, in case your webmaster or someone else tries to talk you into using them. Second, if you're smart about it, many of these techniques can be used in a gray hat SEO campaign.

Keyword stuffing. Before Google, search engines based their results mainly on how many times a keyword appeared on a web page. To improve the site ranking, many websites repeated their keywords hundreds or thousands of times on a page. This is known as "keyword stuffing," and even though search engines have learned how to detect it, some black hat SEO specialists still try to make it work.

No one will want to read a web page that has been stuffed with keywords, so in most cases, the repeated words are in extremely small typeface at the bottom of the page. Sometimes a website owner tries to make the text invisible by using the same color for the text and the page background.

This is one of the most primitive forms of black hat SEO, and search engines caught on to these tricks long ago. Don't let anyone talk you into doing it today—it won't fool anyone.

Tag stuffing. "Tag stuffing" is even more obsolete than keyword stuffing. In the old days, search engines used to look for information called "tags" in the programming of a web page. The tags were supposed to provide clues about the type of information that could be found on the page, but this was an easy opening for black hat SEO. Website owners learned how to attract traffic by putting hundreds of misleading tags on their pages, so most search engines stopped looking at tags years ago.

Cloaking. "Cloaking" a web page means using two versions of it: one version intended for search engine spiders, and the other version intended for human visitors.

The basic concept behind cloaking is that web pages optimized for a search engine can be difficult for humans to read. A site that uses cloaking has a tool to differentiate between spiders and normal users. When a spider asks to look at a page, the website serves up the highly optimized version. When humans ask for the same page, they get a completely different version.

Gateway pages. Imagine you're in your car, looking for a donut shop. You drive mile after mile, getting more and more hungry, until finally you see a new storefront with a donut on the sign. You park your car and walk though the door, but instead of a donut shop, you find yourself standing inside a pawn shop, where some guy walks up and tries to sell you a broken stereo. You'd be a little bit annoyed, wouldn't you?

Black hat SEO operators try to fool internet users the same way, by using gateway pages. A "gateway page" is a page designed to attract traffic from search engine results and drive that traffic to another page or site that has little (or nothing) to do with the keyword its victims were looking for.

Like a cloaked page, a gateway page is optimized to appeal to search engine spiders, so it won't interest most human visitors. The operator of a gateway page hopes that once people arrive at the gateway, they'll proceed to the secondary site without realizing what happened.

Page redirects. Have you ever tried to visit a familiar website only to find that the web address has changed? Often the old page says something like "We've moved to a new address! Our new site will open in your browser in five seconds!" Five seconds later a new page opens without any action on your part. That's known as a "page redirect."

Redirects can be legitimate website actions—a change of web address is a valid reason to use one. When they're used to take visitors from a page they intended to open to a site they don't want to open, redirects are black hat SEO.

Usually redirects are used with gateway pages because most visitors won't willingly open a second page after they land on a gateway page. You won't get a five-second pause with these. Black hat redirects happen as quickly as a visitor's browser allows.

Link farms. "Link farms" came into being soon after Google started counting external links in its ranking system. To repeat what we said earlier, the more pages that link to a given web page, the more important Google (and the other search engines) believes that page to be. A link farm is a collection of unrelated sites designed to take advantage of this fact. Every site in a link farm contains multiple links to the other sites in the farm so they all work together to increase their individual search engine rankings.

Content scraping. "Content scraping" involves creating new web page content by copying fragments of content from other websites. Usually this is done by an automated program similar to a spider. The program searches the internet, evaluates the content on different pages and steals blocks of text for use on a new page.

From a search engine's point of view, the pages created by scraping are full of unique content, so they may qualify for a top place in the search results. Human visitors won't be able to make sense of the content, though, so the pages function only to display ads or as gateway pages to other sites.

Gray Hat SEO

Gray hat SEO, as the name suggests, is a combination of white hat SEO and black hat SEO. Gray hat SEO, like black hat SEO, involves manipulating search engines. Rather than improving the ranking of irrelevant or misleading pages, though, gray hat SEO is intended to improve the ranking of legitimate sites. When you use gray hat SEO, you're trying to fool the search engines, but you're not trying to fool your human visitors.

Gray hat SEO is a good way to get your website in front of more people, but there are risks. Search engines use many automated programs to look for black hat SEO tools, and those programs won't be able to tell you're using the tools for gray hat purposes.

Even if the search engines don't find you out on their own, there's a chance your competitors will see what you're doing and report you as a black hat operator. If that happens, you won't get much sympathy from the search engines. Their terms of use prohibit actions such as cloaking and redirecting. If they learn you're breaking the rules, they won't care why you're doing it. The more prominent you are in your market and the higher your site is ranked, the more likely it is that your competitors will try to get you blacklisted.

That said, if you're careful and you learn how to stay friendly with the search engines, you still may be able to use a few gray hat SEO techniques to your advantage. Cloaking and link farms are the two most reasonable options.

Cloaking. If your website contains a large amount of content that won't be recognized by a search engine spider, you may be able to get away with a little bit of cloaking.

The most common legitimate use for "cloaking" is to let search engines see what's in the members-only section of a membership site. Spiders can't provide useri IDs and passwords, so there's no way for them to access an actual membership site. Since you want the search engine to know what sort of content you make available to your members, the best option is to show spiders a different version of your site, with some of the restricted information on the outside.

Flash animation, Java programming and images are difficult for spiders to read, so if your site contains a lot of that type of content, you may need to describe it in a cloaked page.

As with most gray hat SEO, it's a good idea to get prior approval before you do any cloaking. Let the search engines know which pages you intend to cloak and why you need to do it. This may be difficult, and it may slow down your SEO campaign, but it's much better than getting yourself blacklisted.

Link farms. It's hard to say when a collection of websites crosses the line and becomes a "link farm." Search engines have rules against link farms, but they don't have a good way to detect them, at least not yet.

Since the rules are still being written, stay on the safe side. If you have multiple websites already, you can certainly link them to each other and improve their rankings, but link intelligently. Don't connect multiple pages on sites that have nothing to do with each other, and don't create new websites for the sole purpose of linking them to your existing sites.

Website Promotion

Promoting yourself and your website is one of your most important jobs, and it's what will really give you the edge over your competition.

Everyone who does business on the internet is buying pay-per-click advertising and doing SEO, so the best you can hope for in those areas is to do a better job. However, most business owners, including most information marketers, fail to promote their websites through articles, blogs and discussion groups. Those are great sources of web traffic, and you'll gain an enormous advantage by using them.

Blogs

Every website needs a blog. Adding one to your website will increase your search engine ranking and generate additional organic traffic.

When your blog readers read an interesting post, they'll send some of their friends or business contacts a link to the post. If those people find the post interesting as well, they'll want to know more about the person who wrote it.

Since your blog will always provide a prominent link to your landing page, those readers will soon become sales prospects, and some of them will become customers.

Articles

One thing you can never omit from your articles, reports and white papers is a link to your landing page. When you submit articles to a site like **EzineArticles.com**, you never know who might read them and publish them in secondary sources.

Your article might eventually find its way to thousands of prospective customers, but all that activity is wasted if you haven't provided a path back to King Salutation.

Podcasts and Videos

Internet users love to share audio and video files they like. When you create good content and make it available on hosting and sharing sites, you're recruiting volunteers to promote your website for you.

Forums

Many internet discussion forums have thousands of participants, and those participants return to the forums frequently—sometimes several times a day. Find discussion groups that are likely to attract your customers, and post interesting comments. As with any web promotion, always include a link to your landing page after your comment.

Local Directories

The phone book is rapidly losing its importance. Phone companies and publishers keep churning out the yellow books, but more and more people turn to the internet to find local businesses.

If your products or services are targeted toward a specific geographic area, you have to make sure you're listed on all the main internet directories.

Most of the sites listed here offer free basic listings in addition to more prominent or detailed paid listings. Obviously, you should get free listings in all of them—why turn down free traffic? Paid listings are a good idea if you're in a crowded market or if you can pinpoint the areas where your potential customers live.

In addition to these sites, look for smaller local directories and directories devoted to your particular market. They may not have as many users as Google or Yahoo!, but the users they do have are more likely to visit your site.

Google Local Business Center

Google's Local Business Center is a directory that provides information to users searching for business listings on Google Maps and in the normal text-based search engine.

You can't miss a free opportunity to get your name in front of Google's users. No matter what you're selling, go to Google's Local Business Center, enter your business information and follow the instructions to verify your listing.

If it makes sense for your business, you can also pay to add your own flag to the Google map of your area and to get a more prominent listing next to Google's text-based results. Google calls this a "Local Business Ad," and it's part of the AdWords system. To buy a Local Business Ad, look for a link when you're signed into your AdWords account and follow the instructions.

Yahoo! Local and Microsoft Live

Yahoo! and Microsoft offer services similar to the Google Local Business Center, but they don't get as much use, and they're not quite as easy to use.

You can't ignore these two sites, though, so once you're listed in Google's business directory, take the time to get at least a basic listing with Yahoo! and Microsoft.

Craigslist

Craigslist is one of the top 10 websites in the United States, which is pretty impressive when you look at the site. It's just a list of text links, organized into a dozen or so general categories: personal ads, job listings, items for sale and so on. It's not a shining example of the Power of ONE, perhaps, but it does show the value of keeping things simple.

There's a Craigslist site for every state and for most major cities. No matter what you're selling, you can find a place on Craigslist to promote your website, and the listing won't cost you a thing.

Craigslist posts are sorted by date, and some of the subcategories get a lot of use. As soon as you submit your listing, it will start getting pushed to the bottom by newer posts. Renew your listing frequently, but don't get carried away. Craigslist has rules about over-posting, and its users don't hesitate to report abuse.

CitySearch

CitySearch is another source of web traffic for businesses in or near a major city. CitySearch runs a collection of websites that provide business listings in roughly 50 U.S. cities and a handful of international cities. Most listings on CitySearch are for restaurants and bars, but they have categories to fit almost any type of business.

Visit **InternetInfoMarketing Book.com/spy** to learn how to ethically spy on your competitors and gain valuable information on ways to increase traffic to your own site.

CitySearch offers an interesting "pay-per-call" advertising option called Call Connect. If you pay for a Call Connect listing, your ad is assigned a unique phone number, and you pay CitySearch when someone calls that number.

In-House Traffic Sources

You may not realize it, but if you already have an information marketing business, you are surrounded by additional sources of traffic for your website. Just as you can use your offline advertising—radio, print and TV—to generate traffic, you can use your other offline promotional tools to drive people to your website.

Newsletter

If you distribute an offline newsletter to your customers, start dropping hints about your new website, even if it's still in the planning stage. Once your site is up and running, write a feature story about it, including a few screenshots, if possible. From that point on, mention the site and provide your web address in every edition, preferably on every page of the newsletter.

Customers

When you talk to your customers in person or on the phone, you ask them to stay in touch, don't you? Give them another way to do that by telling them about your website.

Unconverted Leads

If you failed to convert a sales lead in an offline presentation, your website can give you a second chance. Send your unconverted sales leads a quick note, fax or e-mail. Ask them to visit your site. You'll convince at least a few

Traffic is the lifeblood of your business. If you want to leverage the expertise of Bob Regnerus's traffic consultants and grow your business faster with less cost than doing it yourself, visit **RoyalTrafficBuilder.com.**

people to change their answers from no to yes, and since your website is doing the work, you won't have to spend extra time or effort making additional presentations.

Remember, always send people to your landing page rather than your home or sales page. No matter how King Enticement convinces a traveler to visit the kingdom, King Salutation is best suited for welcoming the visitor and setting the stage for the other kings to do their jobs.

Info-Marketer Profile

A Salesperson Sheds His "Monkey Suit" and Kisses the Corporate World Goodbye

Daniel Levis' information marketing business is all about the entrepreneurial possibilities of copywriting on the internet. His weekly column, "The Web Marketing Advisor," addresses internet marketing issues with a strong emphasis on copywriting. Another column, "Selling to Human Nature," is more general in nature and helps salespeople learn how to sell more. At the same time, Daniel uses his column to encourage readers to "shed the monkey suit, say goodbye to the corporate world and get into information marketing."

Daniel has a good reason to target salespeople, actually the best reason: he is a former commissioned salesman himself. He used to sell high-tech products to Fortune 500 companies. And that's what led him to shed his own "monkey suit" and join the world of information marketing.

"My first exposure to information marketing was using what I call lead generation magnets, which were essentially white papers that helped CIOs and IT professionals make more informed decisions," Daniel says. "I would write the free reports to generate leads for my sales as an alternative to cold calling. This was about the time voice mail became popular, and I shifted from cold calling to the 'get ➤

---

them to come to you' Dan Kennedy style of marketing."

Daniel didn't yet have an actual information product since there was no price associated with his white papers, but essentially the marketing process was the same, so his transition into information marketing was a natural one. His first marketing efforts were conducted through the mail, but then in 2003, Daniel started using the internet and discovered e-books online.

"I bought several e-books and found them very useful for figuring out the whole internet thing," Daniel says. "It didn't take me long to put two and two together and realize that selling information, particularly online, was a pretty compelling business. I had already effectively slashed my marketing costs to the bone by shifting over to the internet from direct mail, and here were these guys basically selling electrons for $30, $50, even 100 bucks a pop and more, with essentially no fulfillment costs whatsoever!"

Soon, Daniel figured out that information marketing via the internet was the business he had been looking for. "I started experimenting with it, moonlighting," Daniel relates. "Here was a business I could start up for next to nothing and that would allow me to immediately begin generating revenues. Aside from marketing costs, which I already understood and knew how to control, that revenue was nearly pure profit. It still blows my mind to this day because, for years, I'd been wracking my brain looking for a business opportunity that made sense, but I never found anything I thought was serious that didn't involve forking over a huge wad of cash."

Daniel decided to base his business on something he knew how to do and was passionate about: entrepreneurship. Specifically, he narrowed his topic to copywriting for the internet entrepreneur. "I knew there was a starving crowd of other people out there who were equally passionate about this idea. I had direct experience with it because I was watching the world change literally before my eyes. The large corporations I was selling to back in the early 2000s were one by one downsizing their workforces and increasing their outsourcing to smaller firms and offshore, in many cases to independent consultants and contractors," Daniel explains.

In November 2004, Daniel was ready to dive into information marketing full time. He quit his day job and got started. Although Daniel was proficient in marketing and copywriting, he was a complete unknown. Daniel tackled that problem through co-authorship. "I looked for partnerships with people who were already entrenched in that space," Daniel explains. "One of the people I approached was Joe Vitale (**MrFire.com**), and he agreed to co-author an e-book with me."

The story of how "Daniel the unknown" convinced "Joe the successful info-marketer" to joint venture with him is instructive for anyone who wants to break into the industry. Daniel tells it like this:

"In the fall of 2004, Joe was interviewing Dan Kennedy in one of the first tele-seminars I'd ever attended. Joe's interviewing skills and style just impressed the heck out of me. So I e-mailed him and told him what a great job he did.

"Here's what I said: 'You really got Dan to open up because he's usually kind of calculated. But you really got him comfortable in spilling some really great stuff.' Then in the P.S. I wrote, 'And by the way, you're going to just love my new e-book about Robert Collier.'

"Well, Joe just happens to be a huge fan of Robert Collier. So, I asked Joe to take a look at my book and tell me what he thought. I added that it would be really great if he would give me a testimonial if he liked the book. I sent that e-mail, got up from my desk, and had a cup of tea. About 20 minutes later, I went back to my desk and I was just blown away! There was an e-mail from 'Mr. Fire' himself, with a wonderful, glowing testimonial!

➡

"I immediately replied and asked Joe if he would like to endorse my product to his list for a commission or if he would prefer to do a foreword, call it our co-authored e-book, and take a cut of all of the sales from here to forever. Joe e-mailed an endorsement just a few days later, and we made a ton of sales. And I harvested a whole bunch of e-mail addresses of prospects. My business was instantly profitable from that very first month."

Daniel's experience with Joe can be distilled into a few steps:

- Identify someone who is doing what you want to do.
- Determine what heor she is passionate about and build your product around it (in this case it was Robert Collier).
- Sincerely compliment the person on something he or she has done, and then ask for a testimonial of your product.
- If you get the testimonial, offer a "yes-yes" proposition (endorsement of the book to Joe's list or co-authorship).

Daniel has successfully used this process, which he reluctantly calls "parasitic marketing," to achieve other joint venture projects. One of his most successful is *Masters of Copywriting*.

Masters of Copywriting is essentially a compilation of interviews with 44 master copywriters. It includes well-known experts in the field such as Daniel Kennedy, Joe Sugarman, Clayton Makepeace, Bob Bly, Michel Fortin, John Carlton and 38 others. Daniel also included public domain works of deceased authors, such as Claude C. Hopkins and Bruce Barton, whom, Daniel points out, "all of us revere." By associating himself with these copywriting greats, Daniel positioned himself as an expert. In addition, because each of these writers appeals to a unique client base, Daniel was able to reach a larger universe of potential buyers who already knew one or more of the experts featured in the book.

Another benefit of including multiple experts was being able to get those copywriters to agree to drive traffic to Daniel's website about the e-book. "This created a storm all over the subculture of the internet," Daniel grins. "Right about that time, Clayton Makepeace had hired someone to go out and find partners to help him start 'The Total Package,' his own information product business. I guess this guy happened to get an e-mail from one of the people endorsing *Masters of Copywriting*. So he contacted me and asked me to endorse his e-zine to my list, and I said, 'Well, what's in it for me?' He didn't have an answer, so I gave him one: 'Why doesn't Clayton give me an interview that I'll put in my e-book?' That's how I got Clayton in my book," Daniel explains.

Most of Daniel's interviews were conducted via fax and were text-based. "A few people got smart, and they started requesting audio because they knew how much work it is to write," Daniel says with a chuckle, "and I turned the recorded interviews into bonuses to go with my book."

And the benefits of Daniel's *Masters of Copywriting* just keep coming. "Something else really interesting happened once the list started. People actually started approaching me from within that list and started literally begging me to write sales copy for them," Daniel marvels. "Today, I command a fee of $17,500 plus royalties to write a promotion. And I do a lot of marketing consulting at $300 an hour. My latest venture is I'm adding a forced continuity program at the back end of *Masters of Copywriting* to see how that works."

Today, Daniel's business is about one-half consulting and copywriting and one-half back-end sales to his list by endorsing others' products. He has written for Clayton Makepeace, the *Safe Money Report*, *Golden Newsletter*, the New Orleans Investment Conference, *Real Wealth Report*, *Self Stocks Online* and *The Motley Fool*. This broad client base keeps him busy with consulting and copywriting. ➡

Daniel has plans in the works for a new product in which he details a case study of how he took a particular client and helped him double his response to his marketing. "When he first contacted me, I didn't have time to do any copywriting for him. I was too busy with other clients. But I critiqued his copywriting and gave him a 12-page report identifying all of the gaping holes in his marketing and where he was losing conversion," Daniel says.

One thing Daniel does *not* plan to do is put on super conferences and try to build a multimillion-dollar empire. "I'm a guy who just wants to hang around the house in his pajamas working maybe three or four hours a day because I'm pathologically lazy. I'm perfectly content to make a few hundred grand a year. I went to the SuperConference and a bunch of other conferences, and I remember thinking, 'That looks like a lot of work.' Making a couple hundred thousand dollars in your spare time is not a bad opportunity either," Daniel laughs.

For now, Daniel is happy to have permanently hung up his "monkey suit," ditching the corporate world and living life on his own terms. According to Daniel, it takes two things to be able to do what he did.

"First, there's the mindset," Daniel says. "There are literally millions of people working in corporate America that don't understand how fragile their careers are right now. They don't have the entrepreneurial mindset. They've basically been conditioned for decades to have this employee mindset. Number two is the whole concept of what the information marketing business is about. It's about personal selling, it's about copywriting and it's about marketing. You need to learn how to sell a product first and then develop it second."

Chapter 9

Extra Bells and Whistles

CONGRATULATIONS! YOU'VE COMPLETED YOUR STUDIES WITH THE Five Kings, and you now have the knowledge you need to develop and implement an effective internet marketing campaign.

Of course, even when you're running a perfectly good campaign, there's always room to grow, and there are always things you can do to improve your website and your business.

In this chapter, we look at some features that can make your website more interesting and engaging. Some of them, like video content or live chat capability, jump out and grab your visitors' attention. Others, like dynamic scripting and copy enhancements, give you more subtle ways to draw in your visitors.

Don't forget that these features are merely the subjects of the Five Kings. They may be fun and exciting, but they're only useful as part of a complete marketing strategy. If you pay more attention to the extras than you do to your long-term strategy, the subjects will usurp the Five Kings, and your kingdom will fall into chaos.

Video

In just a few years, everything about internet video has changed. What was once a frustrating and rarely used gimmick has become an essential part of the online experience. That has happened for a number of reasons: more people started using broadband internet connections, new software made it easier to create video files, internet browsers made it easier to view video files and video hosting sites like YouTube gave people a new way to share video content. Add it all up and the result was a sudden and dramatic change in website capabilities and user expectations.

As late as 2004 or 2005, you were basically shooting yourself in the foot if you tried to add video content to your website. To provide decent-looking images, you had to use enormous files, which would take forever to open on most of your visitors' connections. If your visitors actually waited for the video to play, there was only a 50/50 chance that it would play correctly. We never would have recommended video content to clients in those days.

Today, the opposite is true. Video files look much better now, and they take up less space. They open quickly over most connections, and the technology has become reliable. Video content has become a staple of news sites, entertainment sites, web portals and social networking sites, and business websites are quickly getting in on the action. In fact, a business that doesn't put video on its website risks falling behind the competition.

Each one of the Five Kings can use video to his advantage. If you're prepared to take the next step with your website, video content will increase your traffic, improve your opt-in rate and boost your sales.

Using Video on Your Landing Page

A good video can accomplish almost everything you need to do on your landing page. It will grab your visitors' attention, form a connection with them, establish your credibility and make your offer and call to action much more compelling. Every time we've helped a client add video to a landing page, the opt-in rate on the page has improved immediately. If you do it right, you can expect the same results.

When you record your landing page video, remember that you only have one goal in mind. You want to convince your visitor to opt in. This isn't a sales video, a product demonstration or a dating video. Give a brief introduction of yourself or your company and then get to the point. State your offer, sell your offer and tell your visitors how to get the offer. Everything else can wait for the sales presentation.

Bob Regnerus's recommended video software is located at **TheLeadsKingVideo Service.com**.

In Chapter 4, you learned that you have to provide explicit directions on your landing page, and video is a great way to do that. When you've made your offer, point your finger at the place on the page where your opt-in form will appear. It may seem silly, but it works.

When your video is ready, place it "above the fold" on your landing page, just below the headline and subheadline. Program it to start automatically rather than requiring the visitor to hit a "Play" button. Keep it short. Anything over three minutes is too long for a landing page.

Using Video in a Sales Presentation

There are a few options for adding video to your sales presentation. The first option is to do the entire presentation as a video, using any of the three basic types of video (see "What Type of Video Should I Use?" below). If you need to do your presentation in a different format, you can still add video in the form of product demonstrations or customer testimonials.

Video testimonials are even more convincing than text-and-image testimonials, for the same reason that landing page video is more effective than landing page text. Video puts a "real person" in front of the visitor, which creates a stronger connection and adds credibility. Some people may doubt that the quotes on your website came from real customers, but very few will doubt the legitimacy of a video testimonial.

It's a good idea to provide additional video content for information-hungry customers. If you have videos of relevant presentations, seminars or interviews you've done, link to them on your sales page. They're a good way to support your presentation, and you've already done the work to create them.

Using Video on Your Order Form

Just as you can use video to show visitors how to opt in on your landing page, you can use it to show them how to complete your order form. An order form asks for more information than a landing page, so you may not be able to walk your customers through the form step by step. Still, you'll help your cause by including a short (under one minute) video that points out the key items on the form.

Your order form video can help overcome last-minute doubts or questions a customer might have before making a purchase. Be sure to work in a summary of the benefits of your product or service, and most important, ask for the sale.

Using Video in a Follow-Up Campaign

Video has a place in your follow-up campaign as well. Include links to relevant video content, such as seminar or interview footage, in some of your follow-up e-mails. If you used these videos in your sales presentation, it's OK to use them again here, but try to provide a few things that your leads haven't seen already. Variety is important, so don't send the same links in every video.

The videos you link to don't necessarily have to be on your website—many businesses post videos on YouTube and other video hosting sites. Even though anyone can post a video on YouTube, putting your video on such a universally recognized site will raise your profile in the eyes of some consumers.

Using Video to Drive Traffic

Search engines give higher rankings to pages they believe will be more appealing to their users, and since internet users love video, search engines love video. Adding video to a page on your site can have a dramatic effect on the page ranking. When you give the video an effective title and use the right tags (see Chapter 8 for a refresher), you'll see even better results.

This is where YouTube can really help you. YouTube is now the second-most-viewed website in the world. It gets twice as many page views per day as Google or MySpace, and it's almost certain to take the top ranking from Yahoo! in the near future. Because it's so popular, search engines give high priority to YouTube videos in their search results. In fact, they've started to put actual videos rather than links to videos on their search results pages.

On top of that, YouTube has its own internal search function, which millions of people use every day. If your video is truly unique and has the right tags, you can get it in front of an enormous audience.

Google owns YouTube, and as with anything related to traffic, it makes sense to start first with the Google system. Still, keep in mind that Yahoo! and Microsoft have their own video hosting services, and their search engines give priority to videos hosted by their own services. If you're putting a video on YouTube, put it on Yahoo! Video and Microsoft's SoapBox as well.

What Type of Video Should You Use?

Once you know how you want to use video on your website, the next step is deciding which type of video to use. We've separated internet video into three categories: poor man's video, professional video and screen capture video. Each type has its own strengths and weaknesses, and you may have a place for all three in your marketing campaign.

Poor Man's Video

One of the best things about video is its ability to create a connection between you and your customer. Poor man's video is especially effective at building that connection. The term "poor man's video" was coined by John Reese of **Income.com** to describe video that appears to be low-budget or homemade. It looks like something your customers might have made themselves, and it will endear you to them and make them more likely to listen to what you're saying.

The best place to use poor man's video is on your landing page. Visitors come to that page without knowing anything about you or your business. For all they know, you could be running a scam operation out of some foreign country that has no law against internet fraud. At the least, they'll come in with doubts about you. If you hit the right note with your landing page video, you'll overcome your visitors' fears and make them feel as though they're dealing with a trusted local merchant.

Poor man's video can be just as helpful in the other phases of your marketing campaign. It's usually the best way to do video testimonials, and it's often the right way to present your sales materials, follow-up content or promotional videos.

Don't let the name fool you, though. You actually may need to spend a fair amount of time and money creating this type of video. The sound quality and picture quality need to be good, or your visitors won't watch it. The trick is not to let your customers see where the money went.

Shoot the video in an office, warehouse or other familiar-looking location. Dress more casually than you would if you were making a sales presentation in person. Avoid using fancy graphics, flashy editing or professional actors.

There's a place for high-budget, professionally produced video, but it can give the wrong impression if it's used at the wrong time. An expensive-looking landing page video might make your visitors suspect that you're trying to dazzle them into making a bad purchase. You want to present yourself as an expert who is looking for the simplest, most direct way to offer your product or service.

Professional Video

Sometimes, a high-budget professional video is the best tool for the job. When we talk about professional video, we mean a video that looks and feels like a commercial you'd see on prime-time TV. It has high production values and a mix of live action and graphics. Poor man's video, by comparison, should look more like a local TV spot or a cable-access show. Professional video is obviously the most expensive type to use, but it can be extremely effective when used in the right place.

When you're more interested in capturing your visitors' attention than in forming a personal connection, professional video is the way to go. Most of the time, this would be in your sales presentation. Your video might be a long-form infomercial, an in-depth product demonstration or a series of high-profile testimonials. In certain instances, professional video might also be the right thing to use on your landing page or in a follow-up campaign, but be sure to weigh the costs and benefits.

As a general rule, the larger your market, the more you can justify this sort of production. Consumers will be suspicious if you appear to spend big dollars to sell to a small group. If you're trying to reach more people and are facing more competition, your customers will expect a more professional-looking presentation.

Screen Capture Video

Screen capture videos are created using software that records the activity on your computer screen and saves it as a video file. When you combine screen capture video with voice-over commentary, you can create highly effective presentations without spending a lot of time or money.

There are two main uses for screen capture software: low-cost sales presentations and how-to demonstrations. To create a sales presentation, start by building a slideshow in Microsoft PowerPoint or a similar program. When the slideshow is complete, play it back and record both the slideshow and a voice-over with your screen capture software. It may not be as flashy as a live-action video, but it's a lot faster and easier, and it may work just as well.

You can use the same technique to create demonstrations that help your customers use your product or your website. If you're selling software or informative DVDs, use your screen capture program to record the steps involved in navigating your DVDs or using your software. If your website's order form is complicated, provide a video on the page that shows customers how to fill it out correctly.

There are several programs that can create screen capture video, including Camtasia Studio, HyperCam and CamStudio. We've found Camtasia Studio to be the most powerful and easiest to use, and that's the software we use to create our presentations.

Making a Good Video

Here are some things to remember about creating good video content, no matter which type of video you're creating or what purpose the video is going to serve.

Keep it in focus. Yes, a clear picture is always important, but we're talking about a clear purpose. Before you start shooting you have to know exactly what your video is supposed to do. Take the time to figure out what you're trying to accomplish, and plan everything with that goal in mind. It's better to create several short videos than one long video on a variety of topics—a subject can serve only one of the Five Kings at a time.

Always include a call to action. Your video is not there to entertain your visitors. It's there to convince them to take the next step in your sales process. Conclude every video by asking the viewer to take a specific action as soon as the video ends. You spent time and money to create your video, so make sure it works for you.

Work from a script, but don't read from the script. Have you ever noticed that some TV news reporters appear to be speaking directly to you while others are obviously reading their lines? The difference is preparation. The good reporters have memorized their reports and are able to deliver them naturally, even though they may deviate from the script by a word or two. The bad ones don't know what they're going to say next, so they read every single word off the teleprompter.

When you're recording your video, follow the example of the good reporter. Rehearse your presentation until you have committed all the key points to memory. When the camera's on, focus on hitting all your points in the proper order, but don't worry about reciting the script word for word. Looking and sounding natural is the most important thing.

Be patient. No one gets a video done on the first take. Be prepared to go through your presentation at least three or four times before you get it right. You won't really know what you want to do until the camera is running—we've found that the first two live takes do more than 20 rehearsals to get the speaker comfortable with the script.

Don't stop to watch the tape after each take. Do it until it feels right, then go back and see if you need to do anything differently.

Again, nothing in this chapter is an absolute must-have. If you don't have a website now, or if your website needs a lot of work, focus on the fundamentals. You'll have time to add the extras when

For a demonstration on how easy it is to add video to your website, visit **InternetInfoMarketing Book.com/video**.

your marketing campaign is on the right track.

That said, video content is rapidly becoming the rule rather than the exception. As soon as you're ready to start enhancing your website, video is the place to start.

The Telephone

It may not be as exciting as video content, but giving your customers the opportunity to talk to you on the phone is a great way to increase your conversion rate. A phone number does wonders to establish your credibility as a business, and it allows customers to put their minds at ease before making a purchase.

Four of the Five Kings can use the telephone to their advantage. For King Salutation and King Consummation, a phone number is almost a must-have. King Presentation and King Perseverance use the phone less frequently, but they do need it in certain situations. King Enticement is the only king who can count on getting his job done without the telephone.

King Salutation uses the telephone to establish credibility. A phone number on a landing page tells website visitors they're dealing with a legitimate business. Consumers have become nervous about internet fraud, and some of your visitors need to be assured that they're not looking at a sham website designed to collect credit card information. Few of them will actually feel the need to call—seeing a phone number on the landing page will be enough to help them relax.

Put the number in a prominent place on your landing page, and use a large, bold font. Obviously, if your landing page asks visitors to call you or visit you in person, you don't have a choice about putting your number on the page. It has to be one of the first things your visitors see.

The other key page for a phone number is your order page. Remember, King Consummation's job is to make it as easy as possible for a customer to make a purchase. Many customers will have one lingering question after a sales presentation, and if your order form doesn't answer that question, what do you want your customer to do? Search through all the other pages on your website, or pick up the phone and get the question answered right away?

Here's the other big reason to put your phone number on your order form: Many consumers still don't feel comfortable buying on the internet. They may be willing to view your sales materials online, but they want to speak to a human being when they get their wallets out.

Two other kings, King Presentation and King Perseverance, use the phone from time to time. Phone conversations help establish that all-important personal connection in a sales process, so King Presentation offers a number when he wants to solicit questions from potential customers. King Perseverance, for his part, occasionally includes telephone calls as part of a follow-up campaign.

If you're already running an information marketing business, you probably already have a customer service line. In that case, putting the number on your website is a no-brainer. Just be sure you have the capacity to handle the additional call volume your website is going to generate.

If you're starting out, you may not be able to offer phone support right away. Few people can afford to start a business with a 24-hour customer service team. Outsourced customer service can be a less expensive option, but it has its own difficulties, and it's still beyond the reach of many small businesses.

Providing your personal phone number is a good idea in some cases, especially when you anticipate fairly low call volume. Another partial solution to the problem is to send your calls to a voice mail system, which asks customers to leave a message and promises a return call in a certain period of time. It's not as good as providing live support, but as long as you return your calls promptly, you'll keep your customers happy.

Live Chat

Live chat is not exactly a new development—it's been a popular online communication tool for more than 10 years. Until recently, however, it was used mostly for personal reasons. Today, more businesses are discovering the potential of live chat to provide customer service and sales support. By adding live chat capability to your website, you'll help four of the Five Kings get their jobs done more effectively.

The benefits of live chat are similar to the benefits of telephone interaction. It confirms there are real people and a real business behind your website. It creates a personal connection between you and your potential customers. It allows visitors to ask questions about your products or services. In addition, live chat provides two unique benefits: It lets you interact with your visitors without drawing their attention away from the computer screen, and it gives you access to a great deal of information about each visitor you chat with.

As with a phone number, the two most important places to offer live chat are on your landing page and your order form. Live chat generates more feedback on your landing page—it's not as personal as talking on the phone, so it feels like a smaller step to people who aren't sure about getting involved with you.

After you add a chat option to your landing page, you'll notice a flood of new questions from your visitors. Most of those questions will have to do with your landing page offer, and they'll tell you whether you need to improve your landing page copy or the offer itself.

On your order form, live chat lets your customers get their questions answered as quickly as possible. They may have questions about what they're buying, or they may have questions about the form itself, but in any case, you want to provide an answer while the customer is still on the page. Activity that takes the customer away, even if it's just for a few seconds to dial the phone, creates an opening for the customer to have second thoughts or get distracted. Live chat helps you avoid those lost sales, and it's the best way to support your ordering process.

In a sales presentation or a follow-up campaign, live chat helps you keep your sales leads engaged. Every time your visitors ask a question or make a comment, you're one step closer to converting them into customers. Provide a live chat option on your sales pages, and mention the availability of live chat in your follow-up e-mails. This goes without saying, but make sure the links in your follow-up e-mails lead to pages where live chat is available.

There are two ways a chat can start between you and your website visitor: You can initiate it, or the visitor can initiate it. You always want to give your visitors the option to start one, of course. If you choose to initiate chats yourself, you have to be careful how you do it—many visitors will be annoyed or intimidated if you ask them to chat at the wrong time. The best time to initiate a chat is when a visitor has been on your landing page for a longer-than-expected time without opting in. Those visitors may be trying to decide what to do, or they may have just spaced out. In either case, an offer to chat will get their attention and give you an opportunity to push them in the right direction.

There's one other unique benefit to using live chat to communicate with your visitors: Your chat software will provide tons of information about where your chat participants are and how they got to your website. As you'll see below in the section on Google Analytics, the

> Live chat, when done properly, is a fantastic way to increase response. Done poorly, it will hurt your response and lose you money. Consider getting trained on the best way to incorporate live chat the Ari Galper way at **TheLeadsKingChat Software.com**.

more information you have about your visitors, the more effective your marketing campaign will become.

If you're interested in adding a live chat feature to your website, take a look at Ari Galper's service. Ari has developed an excellent training program called ChatWise to go along with an excellent piece of software called LivePerson. The rules for live chat are different from the rules for phone or face-to-face conversation, and Ari's system will teach you what to say, when to say it and how to say it.

Pop-Ups

Many business owners are nervous about using pop-ups on their websites, and for good reason. In the late 1990s and early 2000s, pop-up ads were frequent and annoying enough to ruin the experience of using the internet. It didn't take long for internet service providers and software companies to develop pop-up blockers, and today almost every internet user has multiple lines of defense against pop-up ads. Websites that still try to use them face an uphill battle, and if they manage to get around all the pop-up blockers, the only thing they accomplish is alienating their users.

There's another way to use pop-ups on a website, though, and if you do it right you'll engage your visitors rather than driving them away. The difference is in how the pop-ups work and in what they are intended to do.

Old-style pop-ups open in new browser windows, and they usually have nothing to do with the content on the page they popped up on. They're just advertisements for unrelated companies that have paid for the space. It's easy for pop-up blockers to close those new windows before they open, so this type of ad is becoming a thing of the past. Most businesses shouldn't use them anyway, because if visitors do see the ad and click on it, they're taken to a different website, and they may not come back.

The newer kind of pop-up is not a separate window—it's an element of the page it pops up on. Since it always opens on the same page, it has to be integrated with the other content on that page, or it won't make any sense. This is the type of pop-up you should consider using on your website.

The best place to use pop-ups is on your landing page. Used correctly, they'll grab your visitors' attention, give your offer a sense of urgency and bring in responses you would not otherwise have gotten.

Choose your spots carefully—too many pop-ups will drive visitors away. Some landing pages open a pop-up as soon as the page opens, giving visitors the chance to opt in right there in the pop-up box. That's a good idea if you expect many of your visitors to opt in without reading or viewing the other content on your page.

Another option is to use a pop-up after a visitor has been on the page a long time without opting in. You can often spur those visitors to action with a pop-up that reinforces the value of your offer and gives a clear call to action. However you use them, keep your pop-ups fairly small, and don't use loud colors or lots of animation. Think of a pop-up as a nudge rather than a shove.

If you want to use yet another pop-up on your landing page, use it to make one final appeal as visitors click away. Some people may be annoyed by having to click twice before they can leave, but these are people who have already chosen not to opt in, so you have little to lose. Make this pop-up a little larger and more strongly worded, and you may convince some of your visitors to take another look at your offer.

Most pop-ups today are programmed in Flash, and your web programmer should have no trouble adding them to your landing page. As with any change to your website, stay involved in the process. You have to be sure the timing and placement of the pop-up are right, or you'll create the wrong effect.

Peel-Aways

A "peel-away" is another type of Flash element that you might want to include on your landing page. It makes the page seem to peel away at one corner, revealing another behind it. The only situation in which a peel-away really makes sense is when a visitor attempts to navigate away from your landing page without opting in.

As with a pop-up, you may annoy some people by making them take two steps to leave your site, but those people weren't going to come back anyway. A peel-away gives you one last chance at people who decline your offer, and it won't get in the way of those who do opt in.

Dynamic Scripting

Dynamic scripting allows you to personalize a webpage, making it appear that the page was written specifically for the person viewing it. It's called "dynamic" scripting because the programming changes depending on the input your website receives. This is a great way to build a connection with your visitors, and it's another reason you should use a landing page to greet visitors.

Let's say your landing page asks for a visitor's first and last names and e-mail address. When you use dynamic scripting, your website will start to use that information immediately. If you send visitors to an online sales letter after they opt in, the sales letter can begin "Dear Larry" or "Dear Ms. Wilson" instead of "Dear Visitor" or "Dear Valued Customer." You can continue to address your visitors by name as often as you like—you only have to collect the information once.

You can even use dynamic scripting to sell multiple products from one website. Recently, I (Bob Regnerus) helped Bill Glazer set up a website that offers different versions of a sales letter depending on which type of client is looking at the page (a jeweler, a clothing store owner or a gymnasium owner, for example). Those clients come to Bill's website from different links, and his website is able to recognize the type of client by reading the referral URL.

This is not extremely technical stuff, but it isn't something you should try to do on your own unless you're a programmer as well as an information marketer. Tell your web designer you want to incorporate dynamic scripting on your website, and describe the customizations you want to make.

Copy Enhancements

If you're already running an information marketing business, you probably put a lot of work into your sales letters. You don't just type up a few paragraphs in Times New Roman, print the page and throw it in the mail. You use multiple typefaces and eye-catching images to get your customers' attention. You emphasize important words or phrases with circles, arrows, highlighting and other additions to the text. Those copy enhancements work on paper, and they work just as well online. You can make reading your website easier and more enjoyable by using a tool like CopyDoodles (**CopyDoodles.com**) to add visual appeal to your text. The last thing you want is a boring website.

Audio Content

We used to tell clients that if they couldn't add video to their websites, they should at least add audio. We don't say that any more because video content has become as easy to create and distribute as audio, and video is more effective. Most of the time, there's no need to spend time or money recording audio files for your website.

That doesn't mean that you shouldn't use audio you already have, or that you shouldn't create new audio content if it doesn't drain your resources. The Five Kings may rely more on video these days, but King Presentation, King Perseverance and King Enticement still have some use for audio files.

These days, the best place for audio content is in podcasts— downloadable files for your customers to listen to when they're not online. If you have recordings of interviews or presentations that might be of interest to your customers, put them on your sales pages and link to them in your follow-up e-mails. The one advantage of audio over video is that it's more portable, so offer your customers something they can listen to in the car or on the subway.

Google Analytics

Enhancing your website with Google Analytics will make no difference to your visitors, but it will dramatically improve *your* online experience. Google Analytics is a package of web traffic reporting tools that provide a detailed view of how your website is performing, and it would have cost you thousands of dollars a few years ago. Google now provides these tools free of charge to anyone who wants them, and believe me, you want these tools.

To use Google Analytics, all you have to do is sign up for an account. You'll be given a few lines to paste into your website code, and that's all there is to it. If you already have an AdWords account (and you should), there's no need to sign up again. Click the "Analytics" tab when you're logged into AdWords and you'll get the instructions you need.

You'll be amazed at the variety of information you'll get about your site. Google Analytics offers more than 80 reports that tell you where your visitors are coming from, which keywords they searched for and where they go when they leave your site. In addition, you'll see how your visitors are navigating within your website. You'll know which pages they look at and in what order. You'll see which pages they spend the most time on and which pages they come back to for a second look. You'll also be able to track your bounce rate, or the percentage of visitors who leave your site within a few seconds of getting there.

All these things are important to know at the present, but they'll become even more valuable as you change your website and track the results. The more detail you have about your web traffic, the more you'll learn about the effects of your enhancements.

Info-Marketer Profile

Ari Galper Expands His Direct Sales Process Into an Internet Info-Business

Chances are you haven't met a "typical" information marketer. Typical just doesn't describe these unique entrepreneurs who take their own special paths to success. Each one has an interesting story to tell, and Ari Galper, founder of Unlock the Game®, is no exception.

Ari's story begins and ends with education. He earned his master's degree in the field of Instructional Design—the science of adult learning and education.

He applied his education in the corporate world, writing and designing sales training materials for large companies such as UPS. "Whenever the company would roll out a new product or service, my job was to work with the marketing folks to design and develop the sales training skills and product training materials so the sales force could execute them in the field," Ari explains. "I was the 'knowledge transfer' guy. I was the guy they came to and said, 'OK, here's what we're working on for next year. We need the salespeople to be selling this much, selling this to that customer. Help us design a vehicle to train them to do that.'"

Ari worked with sales representatives who were calling on prospects and new accounts, trying to close the sale. "They were hitting the same walls as everyone else," Ari says. He brought in gurus ➥

---

from the outside to help break through some of the problems his sales reps were experiencing, and that's when he realized there was a big hole in the methodology of training salespeople. "I realized that most of the training out there had this mindset that your only goal is to close a sale," Ari says. "When you take that approach with a new customer, they feel like all you care about is your commission, not really helping them."

Even the words a sales rep uses can make a difference, according to Ari. "There can be covert pressure in the words you use, like 'I was calling to follow up' or 'Did you get my stuff so far?' Any kind of momentum like that creates pressure on the customer."

So, Ari invented a new way of thinking called the Unlock the Game mindset. Ari explains: "It essentially replaces the idea of trying to make the sale. It takes the pressure off the person selling (and the person potentially buying) and allows the prospect to say what he's really thinking. The funny thing is, when you let go of trying to make the sale, you make more sales."

After seven or eight years working behind the scenes training sales reps in corporate America, Ari went into the field as a sales rep himself. He became a sales manager with 18 employees happily using his Unlock the Game mindset. Then a new boss came in who, in Ari's words, was "really old school." Ari decided to go out on his own, putting his theory of nonpressured sales to the test. He created his "Unlock the Game" program with a 20-page e-book.

"The book started selling like hotcakes," Ari exclaims, "so I added a video and a CD to it. Now I have my mastery program online (**UnlockTheGame.com**), which has video as well."

Ari's program includes coaching. "We have coaches that work with people over the phone to help them customize their language. The key to this is not only your way of thinking, but also the words you use," Ari says. "If you use certain types of words, it sounds sales-y."

Ari helps his customers overcome the tendency to pressure their prospects by offering three hours of free coaching as part of his mastery program. Part one of his program sells for $597, and Ari offers a payment plan of $57/month over 12 months. Part two, advanced training, sells for $1,297 and includes more one-on-one video with Ari. He recently held a private seminar with 10 clients who have the mastery one program. "They got to pick my brain for a whole weekend," Ari says. The program includes six DVDs, a journal and "action cards" (similar to flashcards) with reminders for reps to keep next to their phones.

People from every industry imaginable buy Ari's coaching, so he began building a library of recorded coaching calls for individual industries. "I have five to six recordings per industry, so when clients come on board, we give them access to the recordings I did for their industry. So, we've actually automated the coaching, and then we have a live coach who works with them after that if they don't have all their questions answered," Ari explains.

Ari started out doing all the coaching himself, but now he contracts coaching to his clients who have mastered his methodology. Ari says, "My customers just really want to help other people because they were suffering like everybody else. They were hitting the phones, getting the rejection, and this solved their problems, so they wanted to learn more and be close to what I'm doing. The nice thing about my methodology is that it's not industry-specific in terms of how you teach it. It's not about *what* you're selling; it's about *how* you're selling. So, the model applies to any industry, and any of my coaches can train anybody to sell anything."

An interesting feature of Ari's products is that customers have instant access to them online, and then a package with the DVDs,

➡

workbook, etc., is also delivered in a box. "We found that people really like that because they get instant gratification and the kit gets in the mail at the same time, so it just feels right," Ari explains. He also plans to add a monthly subscription program.

Unlock the Game is geared toward people who sell over the phone. Ari has a second business called Unlock the Net Game (**UnlockTheInternetGame.com**), which uses his same sales philosophy to increase conversion rates in web-based companies. "Out of 100 people that come to your site, only one or two convert," Ari says. "The way people are solving it now is by buying more traffic. They have a big hole in their business."

Ari's answer to that problem is a bit unusual: "While most internet marketers try to automate everything, I've grown my entire operation based upon the ability of customers being able to talk to a live person on my website." Ari uses online chat tools on his website to monitor the behavior of his users in real time, to identify gaps in the sales process and to talk to people who aren't going to buy. That way, he can find ways to solve their problems so they will be ready to buy.

Ari is offering two products to help his customers use live chat in their internet marketing: a self-study kit for people who want to do it themselves, and a service that puts a chat box on the customer's website, staffed by a call center certified in Ari's Unlock the Game methodology.

Several big players in the industry are realizing the value of having a live person available to talk to website customers. Perry Marshall was Ari's first Unlock the Internet Game client, and Ken McCarthy and Max Silver are also coming on board. "These are some serious players who are realizing that by not having a live person on their websites 24 hours a day, they are losing a lot of money," Ari says. "They never realized it until we offered the

➤

service." The numbers speak for themselves: "We've been on Perry's site for about three to four weeks on his coaching program, and we've generated over $95,000 in new business to him in that period of time," Ari says.

Ari compares website marketing to a brick and mortar store: "Imagine it's like owning a store. Right now, most internet marketing websites are like owners that have the lights off in their stores; they can't see inside. They don't know when someone is coming in, who's coming in, how to talk to people. It's like flying blind. So, now we're turning the lights on for the first time, and it's a whole new source of revenues they weren't making before."

Giving online customers access to a live person provides the nudge some buyers need to make the purchase. "People need the human touch because they're skeptical," Ari explains. "You go to a website, see a sales letter and a headline, and what are you thinking? Sales pitch, right? That in itself is a turnoff for a lot of people, and unless you have a human being there who can connect at a human level, you're just losing money. There is a segment of the population out there that will not buy unless they talk to a human being, especially if the price point is over $100," Ari says.

The beauty of Ari's business is that he can live wherever he wants, and for now that's in Sydney, Australia, with his wife and two sons. The San Diego native met his Aussie wife online while she was working in Los Angeles. They moved to Sydney because of her large extended family. "My business was pretty much automated online; we've been in Sydney for two and a half years without any business issues," Ari says. He has a staff of three working in the United States who can run the business around the clock for him. "No boundaries!" Ari laughs.

Chapter 10

Getting It
Done

W HEN I (ROBERT SKROB) ATTENDED MY FIRST DAN KENNEDY seminar, I was already a successful entrepreneur. I'm a qualified CPA, and I own Membership Services Inc., a Florida-based association management company. I'd purchased Dan Kennedy's marketing kit a few years earlier, and I'd used Dan's strategies to improve my marketing and copywriting skills. I signed up for a seminar in April 2002 because I wanted to learn more about one of Dan's specialties: information marketing.

Bill Glazer gave the keynote address at that seminar, and he shared the fundamental truth about information marketing: that anyone can make money by packaging knowledge and selling it to the right market. I bought Bill's sales kit and took it home, thinking that I might have found the right new opportunity.

In May, a month after the seminar, I was convinced. I'd read everything in Bill's sales kit, examined the product templates and made my decision: I was going to start an information marketing business of my own.

In July, I was still convinced I wanted to become an information marketer, but I hadn't done anything about it. So I made a new commitment to the idea and set aside two hours every morning to work on my new business.

For the first three weeks, everything went well. In those two hours per day, I was developing outlines, designing templates and making plans for an amazing set of information products. I started working on a number of how-to manuals, and I finished one of them before the project ran out of steam. I still had a full-time business to run, after all, and there were too many distractions. The information marketing business went on the back burner.

The following May, I signed up for another seminar. The night before the seminar, I got together with a handful of other marketers to share stories and ideas. One of the people I met that night was a college sophomore who had been in the audience for Bill Glazer's information marketing speech the previous April—the same speech I had heard.

Like me, this young guy had bought Bill's sales kit and decided to start a new business after attending the seminar. Unlike me, he had made $150,000 as an information marketer in the past 12 months.

I couldn't believe my ears. Here was a kid with no real business experience, no office, no employees and limited connections, and he had created a booming business in one year's time. I had all the tools I could possibly need, and I had done next to nothing as an information marketer.

What was the difference? While I had spent weeks and months working on one piece of the puzzle, this kid had jumped in with both feet right away. The first thing he had done was to promote his new business and find potential customers. Then, when he had generated interest, he created his sales presentation. It only took one weekend to get it done. After he had taken his first few orders, he got around to creating his product. That step also took a single weekend—he couldn't afford to put it on the back burner because he had customers waiting.

I knew it was risky (legally and otherwise) to take orders for a nonexistent product, but I couldn't argue with the kid's results. I realized I needed to try a more aggressive approach if I ever wanted to get my own business off the ground.

The next time around, I started by getting in touch with my potential customers and establishing myself as a trusted source of information. Then, when I had my product ready for the market, I already had people to sell it to.

This turned out to be the winning formula, and I've used it to start several lucrative businesses since 2003. It's also the best way to kick-start your own career in information marketing.

The Official Internet Information Marketing Checklist

Ready to get started? The Official Internet Information Marketing Checklist walks you through the process of building your internet information marketing campaign from start to finish.

❑ **Identify Your Market**. Find out what your target customers want to know. Try to understand their problems and frustrations. What information do they need?

❑ **Connect with Your Market**. Start a blog and write a post or two every day about topics your customers will find interesting. Ask questions and encourage your readers to post their answers in the "Comments" section of your blog.

Establish your identity in your market by writing articles, reports and white papers and submitting them to clearinghouse sites.

❏ **Create Your Product**. Eventually, you may want to offer dozens of products or services, but in the beginning, you only need one. Use what you've learned on your blog or in conversations with potential customers to create your solution to the problem.

You can move to the next steps on this checklist while you work on your product, but at the very least, you have to know what you're going to sell before you can build a website to sell it.

❏ **Create Your Lead Offer**. In addition to your main product or service, you're going to need a smaller offer to get responses on your landing page. You can use a limited piece of your main offer, or you can create something entirely new. Remember that this offer must appeal to your sales prospects, and it must leave them wanting more.

❏ **Plan Your Sales Funnel**. Figure out how you're going to close sales. Will you have an online store, or will you generate leads online and then follow up with offline sales materials?

If you already have an information marketing business, figure out how your website fits into the big picture.

❏ **Plan Your Website**. Look at your sales funnel and determine what you need to get from your website. Is it sales, or is it sales leads? Once you have your answer, build a flowchart to map out each step of a visitor's experience on your site.

Remember what you've learned about the Power of ONE, and plan a website that presents your visitors with one yes-or-no decision at a time.

❏ **Create Your Landing Page**. This is the most critical step in the entire process, so be sure to follow all King Salutation's rules for landing pages. Be sure you have each of the following elements on your page:

- The right domain name
- A clear headline
- Good copy
- An appealing offer
- A call to action
- Credibility
- Multimedia content
- Effective design and layout

❑ **Create Your Sales Presentation.** Whether you're using an online sales letter, a multimedia presentation, a tele-seminar or a Shock-and-Awe package, your sales presentation must do the following five things:

- Describe the problem.
- Describe the solution.
- Separate your solution from the competition's.
- Justify your price.
- Inspire immediate action.

❑ **Create Your Order Form.** Your order form is more than a page to collect credit card numbers. Follow King Consummation's seven laws for effective online order forms:

- Use a benefit-driven headline.
- State the benefits.
- State the deliverables.
- Offer choices and terms.
- Re-establish your credibility.
- Remove risk.
- Provide instructions.

❑ **Create Your Thank-You Page.** A thank-you page is the best way to conclude the sales process. After thanking your customers for their business, repeat the key information about their order and use the momentum to offer another product or service.

❑ **Write Your Follow-Up E-Mails.** Sign up with an autoresponder service and write a series of at least seven e-mails to send to your unconverted sales leads. Remember the Six Laws of King Perseverance:

- Timing is everything.
- Keep it short.
- Keep it personal.
- Ask questions.
- Include a call to action.
- Use offline tools.

❑ **Start Driving Paid Traffic.** Build your keyword list, starting with the obvious search terms and adding more unusual ones as you gather information.

Sign up for a Google AdWords account, and start driving traffic to your site with pay-per-click advertising. Once you have the hang of it, start advertising with Yahoo! and Microsoft as well.

Continue to expand your advertising campaign with banner ads, affiliate programs and paid directory listings. That way, you protect yourself against sudden changes in the world of online advertising.

❑ **Start Driving Organic Traffic.** Optimize your website for maximum search engine visibility. Use all the white hat SEO strategies described in Chapter 8, and carefully add a few gray hat strategies.

Don't forget to list your site in free business directories and encourage your existing customers to visit your site.

> Continue to expand your promotional campaign by posting to your blog, submitting articles and participating in discussion groups.
>
> ❑ **Add Extra Features**. If you didn't include video content when you built your site, add it as soon as possible. Other features, such as live chat, telephone support and dynamic scripting, create a closer connection between you and your website visitors.
>
> ❑ **Track Your Results**. Use Google Analytics and your own web traffic logs to track the performance of your advertising, landing page, sales presentation, order form and follow-up e-mails. Testing and analysis are critical to the success of every internet marketing campaign.

Who's Going to Do the Work?

Now that you know exactly what you need to do to get your internet information marketing business up and running, there's only one question left to answer: Who's going to do the work? Are you going to do it yourself, or are you going to hire someone to do it for you?

Doing It Yourself

There's only one real benefit of building your website on your own, but it's an important benefit: minimal cost.

Remember Tracey and Dan from Chapter 1? They're the couple who built a thriving information marketing business and spent $47 to do it. If you use the strategies you've learned in this book, you can expect to see the same sort of results with a similar initial investment.

The dollar cost is only one part of the equation, of course. There are two other factors to consider.

The first is time. Tracey spent a few hundred hours writing her candle-making book, and Dan spent a few hundred more building and improving a website to sell the book. From the day Tracey had the idea to write a book to the day they closed their first sale, almost a full year went by.

The other factor you have to consider is expertise. Tracey knew all about making candles, so she was qualified to write a book about it. Dan, on the other hand, didn't know much about web design, landing pages or pay-per-click advertising. He stumbled a bit at first, but he was able to learn along the way, and after a few months of work, the money started to roll in.

If you don't have money to spend, you can follow Tracey and Dan's example and do everything yourself. Nothing you've learned in this book is out of reach, if you're willing to learn a few new skills and put in the hours to make everything work.

If you have a budget, but you're short on time or expertise, you might want to consider outsourcing some or all of the work.

Getting Outside Help

Of the 15 items on the Official Internet Information Marketing Checklist, only the first one—Identify Your Market—is something you have to do yourself. You can hire people to handle the other tasks for you. In fact, if you're willing to spend the money, you can outsource all 14 of them at once.

Below are some general tips on outsourcing the different phases of an internet information marketing campaign. For a list of reputable vendors, see the resource guide on **InternetInfoMarketingBook.com**.

Outsourcing Your Content

If you want to get into a market that you don't know much about, if you don't have much faith in your writing skills or if you simply don't have the time to sit down and write a book, you can hire writers to create your content for you.

I used this strategy when I started my first information marketing business. Before I got started, I knew that I wanted to try marketing on the internet, but I wasn't sure what type of information I should sell. To identify my market, I set up a series of websites and asked visitors to submit questions on various topics.

I kept an eye on those websites and discovered that there was a large demand for information on the subject of candle-making. This was years before I met Tracey and Dan, by the way. Luckily for us, there was enough room in the market for two information marketing businesses.

After doing my research, I had identified my market, and thanks to the website I was running, I had already developed a connection with that market.

The next step was to create my product, and that's where I was stuck. I knew I wanted to sell an e-book online, but I didn't know the first thing about candle-making. I didn't have the time or interest to learn about it and then write a book. The answer was hiring a writer to do it for me. I solicited bids on a site for freelance writers and found someone willing to write a 120-page book on candle-making.

I sent my writer the list of questions I had collected, and six weeks later, I had my book. It cost me a few dollars, but I considered it money well spent. The book was a success, and I applied the same strategy several more times in different markets.

You can use outside writers to do more than create your product. If you're not an experienced marketer, it may be well worth the money to hire professional copywriters for your landing page copy, your sales presentation and even your pay-per-click ads.

Outsourcing Your Website

Building and running a website is a multistep process. If you aren't planning to do the work yourself, you may need to hire vendors to handle each element of the process:

- **Development**: Determine the basic structure and programming of your website.
- **Design**: Plan the visual appearance of your website, including the background, images and text layout.
- **Multimedia creation**: Record audio, video or animated content for your website.
- **Order processing**: Collect payments from your customers and deliver electronic products after a sale or opt-in. In many cases, you'll need one service to collect the information and a secondary service to process the credit card transaction.
- **Advertising**: Create your pay-per-click and banner ads, and manage your accounts with the various ad services.
- **SEO**: Optimize your website for maximum search engine visibility.
- **Follow-up**: Send e-mails to your existing customers and unconverted leads. Your autoresponder may be able to handle some aspects of order processing as well as your follow-up campaign, or you may need two services.

No matter which tasks you decide to outsource, always get referrals and look at the work your vendors have done for previous clients. Prices for many of these services have dropped dramatically in the last few years, so don't be afraid to shop around.

Hiring a Consultant

As you can see, there are a lot of smaller jobs involved in getting an internet information business off the ground. Depending on your budget, you might want to do it all yourself, or pick and choose certain tasks for yourself and outsource the others. The last (and most expensive) option is to hire a consultant to manage the entire process for you.

An internet marketing expert can drastically speed up the process of creating your website and generating traffic. If you hire the right person, you'll get better, faster results, and you'll free yourself (and your employees, if you have them) to focus on your own area of expertise.

A good consultant will help you develop your strategy and evaluate your results. You may not know whether a 9 percent opt-in rate on your landing page is good or bad, but your consultant should, and if you need to revise your page, your consultant should know where to start.

If you're interested in hiring an internet marketing expert, ask lots of questions. You need to know whom your candidates have worked for and what results they've achieved. Ask about their experience in your industry or market, and find out if they have connections who can help with other elements of your campaign.

Use this book as your guide when you interview potential consultants—you should only hire someone who can speak intelligently about every topic we've covered here.

It isn't for everyone, but if you have the resources, hiring an expert consultant is the best way to bring your internet information marketing business to life.

Start Today, Not Tomorrow

This book has provided all the information you need to start selling information on the internet. The only difference between you and a successful internet information marketer is that you're not doing it yet. But you're about to change that, aren't you?

There's no reason to put it off. Learn from Robert's example and start connecting with your market today. You can create your website, your sales materials and even your product as you go along. The longer you wait to get started, the longer it will be before you close that first sale.

We have a special video that will help you get started if you visit **InternetInfoMarketingBook. com/bobandrob.**

Appendix A

Glossary of Info-Marketing Terms

Here are common terms you'll hear in the information marketing business.

AdWords Short form of *Google AdWords*, which is the pay-per-click advertising platform for Google.

Affiliate A relationship in which there is an agreement between two people to sell a particular product. One individual has customers he wants to market the product to, and another one has the product or service he wants to offer to customers. Typically, the individual who has the product will create an affiliate program. Many of these are executed online, and most of the popular shopping cart software programs today have this feature built in. The affiliate completes an application. On approval of the affiliate relationship, the affiliate is assigned a unique website address and given access to the affiliate toolbox with e-mails, websites, ads and other things the affiliate can use to help sell the program. Then the affiliate uses the link and uses those sales techniques to sell the product, and an affiliate commission is paid on those products. Commissions vary substantially by the different products and services sold. Very often the terms are negotiable for individuals who can sell a lot of affiliate programs, but for most folks, you normally have to earn a higher commission rate by performing well for a particular affiliate.

Affinity A measure of your relationship to a market. If you have been a member of a market for a number of years, perhaps having established a career there, then you would have a high affinity with that particular market. If you are new to a market (for example, if you are going to sell to Harley-Davidson owners, you've never owned a Harley and you don't know anyone who owns one), then you would have little affinity with that market.

Alexa.com A website that allows you to gather information about competitors and about websites in a particular market. It provides a lot of information about the site, including how much traffic it's receiving from the internet.

Autoresponder A computer program that automatically answers e-mails sent to it. Autoresponders are used as e-mail marketing tools to immediately provide information to prospects and then follow up with them at preset intervals. Autoresponders are also incorporated into electronic mailing list software to confirm subscriptions, unsubscriptions, posts and other list activities.

Back end The most profitable part of an information marketing business and what distinguishes info-marketers from all other types of information publishers. Info-marketers are able to sell coaching, consulting, seminars, automatic implementation products and newsletters, and offer other people's products to their customers as additional revenue opportunities.

Churn Refers to the number of members joining a market at a given time. For instance, the real estate agent industry is a market where there is a lot of churn. Many individuals are joining that market with the hopes of making lots of money as real estate agents. In contrast, the funeral director industry has very little churn. Most of the entrants in that market have been family-owned businesses for many years, or they are large corporations buying the family-owned businesses. There are not a lot of companies jumping into the funeral director business that were not in it 12 months ago.

Claims The benefits you are telling potential customers they'll receive from using your product. *Income claims* refers to the amount of income you state others have received from using your product.

ClickBank A website service that allows information marketers to sell electronic books without the hassle of setting up a merchant account and electronic order-taking.

Coaching An arrangement where you provide advice and counsel to customers to help them implement their own problem solutions. You may have already provided them the information they need, but through a coaching program, you are able to give them specific information for their particular problems as well as specific case examples to help them solve the problems. This is generally distinguished from consulting. Consulting is actually doing it for them, whereas coaching is helping them to get it done for themselves.

Continuity A program where, at an established interval (usually monthly), customers are charged a set fee for a given level of product and service. Most programs are on a monthly continuity. This concept was pioneered and made popular by the Book-of-the-Month program, where customers trusted a publisher to send them a book every month related to their interests. This created an ongoing continuity relationship between these customers and the publisher. Info-marketers have used continuity to revolutionize their businesses and add many more subscribers versus using the annual subscription model. (See *Forced continuity*.)

E-book A book in a digital file that communicates information to your prospects and can be delivered electronically over the internet. Rather than printing a product, weighing it, putting postage on it and mailing it, you are able to instantly deliver an e-book and put your product in the customer's hand immediately.

E-mail list An electronic mailing list that allows for widespread distribution of information to many users at once. Similar to a traditional mailing list—a list of names and addresses—as might be kept by an organization for sending publications to its members or customers.

Endorsed mailing A mailing where an individual is given a letter of endorsement, usually a brief letter added to the front of a sales message, that gives credibility and recognition to the offer and sales message that it would not have gotten if it had to stand on its own.

Follow-up e-mail Messages sent via e-mail to subscribers after they opt in to a mailing list.

Forced continuity An arrangement where the customers are provided a free trial period of a program, at the end of which they are automatically added to the continuity program. It does not require customers to act to opt in to the monthly continuity. Customers can always opt out if they choose; however, they do not have to act to opt in. (See *Continuity*.)

Front end Marketing your products and services to new customers. The first step of your info-business. After you're able to obtain customers through your front end, you can develop the back end of your business by selling additional products and services to the customers who have already made a purchase from you.

Group coaching A model where, instead of the coach interacting with one student at a time, the coach interacts with many students at one time. In general, a coach is providing advice and counsel, examples and encouragement to students, and is not performing actual services for the students. In the group coaching environment, there are many students interacting at the same time with one or more coaches.

Guarantee Your assurance to your customers that your product is everything you say it is. You promise to stand behind your product and offer their money back if your customers are dissatisfied with it.

Guarantee, conditional A guarantee where you force the customers to go through certain hoops to receive their money back. They may have to implement certain features within your product to demonstrate that they've tried some things before you will give them a refund.

Guarantee, unconditional A guarantee where the customers can simply ask for the refund, and they are given it with no conditions whatsoever.

Herd Term coined by Dan Kennedy to refer to an info-marketer's customer base. Expanding on the herd analysis, Dan teaches info-marketers to build fences around their herds to protect them against poachers and to prevent customers from escaping.

Joint venture Where two or more individuals collaborate to create and market a product to a particular industry. In many cases, one of the joint venture partners has a list of customers, and the other joint venture partner has a product or will develop a product or service for those customers. The partners work together to sell the product and split the proceeds.

Kit A collection of materials you're delivering all at one time to your customers.

Landing page A page that appears when a visitor clicks on an ad. The page contains a single objective for generating a specific response.

Lead generation The process of identifying individuals in a market who are interested in more information about the product or service you offer.

Market A collection of customers who have something in common and, most important, have a common problem you can solve as an info-marketer.

Mastermind meeting The ideas of the "mastermind alliance" and "masterminding" grew from Andrew Carnegie, Henry Ford, Harvey Firestone and Thomas Edison, as reported in books such as the popular bestseller *Think and Grow Rich* by Napoleon Hill. One of the factors that successful people share is a group of people with whom they can work to solve problems. By working together to solve each other's problems, all benefit. Many information marketers have been able to duplicate the benefit of mastermind meetings through their coaching programs.

Monthly CD An audio or other program offered through podcast or other means that individuals subscribe to. They can be provided by one person as a monologue, or they can be in a conversation or interview format between an expert and a host.

Multipay An arrangement where the info-marketer helps customers afford the product by offering a payment program. It can be two-pay, three-pay, five-pay, etc., but this helps lower the initial price of the product and decreases the risk that customers may perceive from the sale. For example, if a customer looks at an offer that is $250 a month for four months, it may seem more acceptable than a single payment of $1,000, even though he or she could probably self-finance that $1,000 through a credit card. It feels like $250 is all the customer is risking, so he or she is more apt to participate in a multipay program than in an all-upfront sale.

Newsletter A publication that's produced, usually monthly, by an information marketer to communicate with customers, to provide ongoing help and information, and to reinforce what the info-marketer has taught them.

Niche A group of individuals with a like interest or a similar demographic. Normally these niches are defined as business-oriented—the customers could be plumbers, restaurant owners, chiropractors, doctors or accountants, for example.

Offer What you agree to provide your customers for a fee. Most teachers in the info-marketing world will tell you your offer is the most important part of your marketing campaign. You should create a compelling offer even before you create a product, a collection of resources, tools, techniques, manuals, CDs, videos, coaching: whatever you want to package in your offer. Then you can create the product and offer it to the marketplace.

One-step sale A process where you go straight from introducing yourself to the customer to asking for the sale, all in one marketing piece. Contrast this to lead generation marketing, where you first generate a lead through a lead generation ad and then create a sales sequence to sell to that lead. Through one-step sales, you sell at the point of first contact.

Online marketing A method of using the internet to communicate with many people via automated software that handles the lead capture, marketing and sales process as well as product delivery.

Opt-in When someone is given the option to receive more information via e-mail. Typically, this is a mailing list, newsletter or advertising.

Opt-in, unconfirmed A new subscriber first gives his or her address on a web page, but no steps are taken to assure that this address actually belongs to the person.

Opt-in, confirmed (COI) A new subscriber asks to join a mailing list, but unlike unconfirmed opt-in, a confirmation e-mail is sent to verify it is really that person. Some marketers call this *double opt-in*.

Order form Also called a *response device* or *application*. A piece of paper, the document or the web form the customer uses to make a transaction. This is where the customer enters his or her name, address and credit card information. The order form is mailed, faxed or completed online or on the phone. If completing a phone order, the person taking the order usually has an order form to complete for the customer.

Pay-per-click (PPC) An advertising model used on search engines, advertising networks and content websites/blogs where advertisers pay only when a user clicks on an ad to visit the advertiser's website. Advertisers bid on keywords they predict their target market will use as search terms when they look for a product or service. When a user enters a keyword query matching the advertiser's keyword list or views a page with relevant content, the advertiser's ad may be shown. These ads are called a *sponsored links* or *sponsored ads* and appear next to or above the natural, or organic, results on search engine results pages or anywhere a webmaster/blogger chooses on a content page.

Prerecorded message A message, usually through a toll-free number, that you offer in your lead generation ad to encourage your customers to leave their names and contact information so you can deliver the rest of your sales message to them.

Reachability Refers to a niche describing the ease with which you can put your marketing message in front of your prospective customers. If a niche already has several magazines, others already marketing there or its own cable television channel, then that market is highly reachable. If there are no magazines specific to that niche, then its reachability is low.

Response device See *Order form.*

Risk reversal A marketing term for a guarantee with which you ease a customer's fear of making a purchase by taking on all the risk of the sale. As customers evaluate whether they wants to buy your product, they are deciding whether they can trust you. By offering to refund the purchase price and pay for return shipping if the customer returns the product, you are taking on all the risk of the sale. This helps your customer buy from you with confidence.

S&D (steal and distribute) Term coined by Bill Glazer. Rather than reinventing ways of doing business or new marketing programs for a particular niche, you adapt programs that have proven themselves successful in other areas and implement them in your own market.

Self-liquidating leads When your lead generation ad charges the potential customer a fee to receive the rest of the marketing sequence. For example, the ad has an offer, invites people to respond and charges them $9.95 to get the rest of the marketing sequence. This type of lead has two benefits: It provides income from the lead generation process that helps pay for more lead generation ads, and it increases the quality of the lead because, even though it's a nominal fee, only the most motivated individuals are willing to go through the effort to respond. When you use a free lead generation system and all people have to do is pick up the phone, you dramatically increase the number of leads you get and the number of opportunities you have to sell to individuals. You also increase your marketing cost.

Squeeze page A web form that captures a name and address from a prospect before you allow the prospect to see the rest of the sales message. (See *Landing page.*)

SRDS (Standard Rate and Data Service) A manual containing details about every list commercially available for sale. From the

SRDS manual you can learn about markets based on the types of lists available for them and evaluate how easy it would be for you to reach this market through direct mail.

Subculture A way to evaluate a potential market. While niches are based on professional designations, such as doctors and plumbers, subcultures are based on hobbies and interests of particular individuals. Golfers, fishermen, Star Trekkies, bird lovers—all are subcultures you can market to.

Subniche Specialties within a particular niche. For example, a plumber could be a commercial plumber who works only in 30-story buildings, or he could be a residential plumber. There are many subniches for doctors: dermatologist, surgeon, gynecologist, anesthesiologist.

Tele-coaching A process of delivering coaching services over the phone rather than in person or by mail.

Telemarketing A process of delivering a sales message over the phone.

Tele-seminar A seminar delivered over the phone. Most tele-seminars offered by information marketers are free and provide a sales presentation. The sales presentation can be for a tele-coaching program as a back-end product. Many info-marketers use tele-seminars to convert sales on the front end. Not only do they offer printed sales letters and CDs, they also invite their leads to call into a tele-seminar to hear a sales presentation.

Tollbooth position Once you have developed a list of customers, there are other individuals who want to sell products and services to your list. Because you have a relationship with your list, you are in a position to charge others for access to your customer list, either through an affiliate program, a JV opportunity, an endorsed mailing or some other agreement.

Try-before-you-buy Often called a *puppy dog close* because it was borrowed from the pet stores that allow you to take a puppy home for the evening. Once you have taken a puppy home, gotten used to him, shown the puppy to your neighbors and friends and taken him for a walk, the likelihood of returning the dog to the store is low. An info-marketer may offer a try-before-you-buy where the customer is able to complete an order form, fax it in, receive the product, and examine it for 30, 60 or 90 days, and then the charge goes through automatically if the customer has not returned the product.

Wordtracker (TheLeadsKingKeywordSoftware.com) A website that lets you find out exactly how many people are searching for particular keywords and phrases. When you're trying to determine how to position your product within a market, you can examine the types of keywords and phrases individuals are searching for on the internet. That will give you an idea of what you should offer them.

Appendix B

Info-Marketing Resources and Vendors

O NE OF THE TOUGHEST PARTS OF THE INFORMATION MARKETING business is finding vendors who understand what you're trying to accomplish and are able to get you there. Too many fail to deliver. An info-marketer must be able to act quickly. Once you get new customers, incompetent vendors can kill a business.

Here are vendors who understand info-marketers and are ready to help you become successful.

Customer Service

Turn-Key Customer Service, Marketing Implementation and Product Fulfillment

To streamline their businesses, smart info-marketers have outsourced all this time-consuming work to Sheiff Services. Randy and Camille Sheiff are in the office each day, supervising a call center, managing an

InfusionSoft ManagePro CRM system for their clients and making sure orders are filled and customer service questions are handled promptly.

In fact, because they're doing this, their info-marketer clients are able to start up their businesses more quickly, get more marketing steps implemented and generate more money without additional effort. In addition, info-marketers don't have to deal with the dozens of customer questions that come in each day.

For more information about how Randy and Camille Sheiff can take over the administrative hassles of your info-business, call Randy at **(512) 353-5037.**

Business Marketing/Management System

A Software System That Puts Your Info-Marketing Business on Autopilot by Automating Your Marketing, Sales and More

Are you tired of never being in control of your prospect and customer information? Does your business suffer because you use three, four or five software programs to manage your business? We understand your pain, and we have a web-based CRM Software program built specifically for your info-marketing business.

ManagePro CRM is your customer relationship management system. Finally you can place your customers at the center of your business where they should be. All your customer interaction via e-mail, phone, fax or in person is tracked and managed in one place so you can close more sales and maintain better relationships with your existing customers.

No more trying to track which leads are in which step of multiple marketing sequences. ManagePro CRM lets you *supercharge* your follow-up sequences. In addition to sending follow-up e-mails, ManagePro CRM will send direct mail pieces, faxes, voice broadcasts and more—automatically.

For a free product tour, autoresponder test drive and online demonstration, visit **TheLeadsKingCRM.com.**

Legal Services

Build Your Business, Protect Your Assets

We'll tell you how we can help your information marketing business get off to a fast start! Call Nevada Corporate Planners Inc. at **(888) 627-7007** for information and fees. Or e-mail us at **NCP@NVinc.com.**

Successful Info-Marketing Business Startup

Garrett Sutton is a corporate attorney advising small business owners. As one of only three Rich Dad's Advisors, he teaches corporate formation and business finance strategies to thousands of new business owners each year. He has written several bestselling books, including *Own Your Own Corporation* and *How to Buy and Sell a Business*. He also hosts a syndicated internet radio show, *Wealth Talk America* (**WealthTalkAmerica.com**). His firm provides asset protection and business-building services to thousands of clients around the country and internationally. For more information, visit **BusinessCreditSuccess.com.**

The Business Growth Lawyers

In the speed of today's business world, actionable information creates opportunity. Opportunity creates a position for unique revenue streams and fast, high-margin profits to the person or company that controls the flow of information. Naturally, opportunities of this magnitude get the focus of government regulators, and enterprising info-marketers need sound legal advice to navigate the complex mix of legal disciplines.

Info-Marketing Law is a legal practice that connects the diverse disciplines of intellectual property, contract law, franchising, business opportunity, consumer protection, FTC regulation, corporate securities, business law and internet law, blending them into a specialty for the information business. For more information, visit **NicksNanton.com**.

Publicity Tools

Free Publicity, Drive Traffic to Your Website

When you use PR LEADS, we **put you in touch with reporters** who need to quote experts like you. That's right. We get approximately 100 requests a day from reporters writing stories for major publications who need to find experts to quote in their stories. We **give you their names** and **e-mail addresses** and **their story angles** so you can contact them. If you have the information they need, they'll feature you and your books in their publications. We're talking big-name publications and media outlets such as *The Wall Street Journal*, **CNN** and *Newsweek* as well as *Redbook* and *Glamour*. For more information, visit **InfoMarketingPRLeads.com**.

Media Duplication

These companies handle duplication for all your follow-up mailings and product fulfillment or duplication jobs. They can produce the duplicates and deliver them to you or ship directly to your customers when you receive orders.

- CD duplication
- DVD duplication
- Cassette duplication
- Complete line of packaging

Corporate Disk Co.

Joseph Foley, phone **(815) 331-6000, ext. 233**, or visit **Disk.com**.

McMannis Duplication

Tony Wedel, phone **(620) 628-4411** or visit **McMannisDuplication. com.**

Merchant Services

A Merchant Services Provider That ...

... appreciates info-marketers, understands the business and wants to help you make more money.

Info-marketers everywhere are shocked to learn that their merchant services provider considers them to be a liability. Even after these providers unconditionally accept your business, they can impose six-month holds on your money without notice, refund your customer charges or cancel your account altogether.

Now there is an alternative. One merchant services provider likes info-marketers and wants your business. For a free, no-obligation evaluation of your current merchant services needs and future opportunities, visit **InfoMarketingMerchantServices.com.** Complete the quick form, and someone will contact you right away.

Merchant Services With Info-Marketers in Mind

Info-marketers: let Charge Today provide you with full-service merchant accounts and credit card processing solutions for today's demanding marketplace.

From merchant accounts, ACH/check services, secure gateways and virtual and physical terminals to shopping carts, **ChargeToday.com** is the info-marketer's premier partner for credit card payment and processing solutions. For more information, visit **ChargeTodayInfo.com.** Complete the brief form, and Charge Today will be in touch with you within 24 hours.

Info-Marketing Technology Tools

The Shopping Cart Used by the Most Info-Marketers ...

... to take orders online, follow up with prospects and run affiliate campaigns.

All the shopping cart and marketing tools needed to automate a successful online info-marketing business. With 1ShoppingCart, info-marketers can take orders online, accept credit cards, e-mail customers, use automatic e-book delivery, use ad tracking tools, have unlimited autoresponders, use discount/update modules and have access to a built-in affiliate program. For more information, visit **TheLeadsKingShoppingCart.com**.

Create Products Fast

We help info-marketers uncover quick-profit niches and uncover what their prospects and customers want to buy "most." With the Ask Database, create new products from scratch, effortlessly grab more testimonials from members, uncover new market niches using Google AdWords and quickly determine winning tele-seminar content. For more information, visit **TheLeadsKingSurveySoftware.com**.

Easy Follow-Up Messages and E-Zines

With AWeber, info-marketers can configure follow-up and newsletter messages with name personalization click-through and open rate tracking, attachments, RSS and split testing at no additional cost. Messages can include HTML using our 51-plus predesigned templates, or create your own with the integrated easy editor and images or plain text. For more information, visit **TheLeadsKingAutoResponder.com**.

Audio/Visual Production

Bayfront Productions

Turn to Bayfront Productions to create high-quality audio and video products. After working with info-marketers for many years, Bayfront Productions knows what info-marketers need to create products and marketing materials.

Miroslav Beck, phone **(813) 810-6241** or visit **VideoMarketing Expert.com.**

Leading Experts TV

One stop to creating a broadcast-quality 30-minute show highlighting you as an expert. Use your video on your local TV station or exhibit booth, or broadcast it as part of sales presentations. Visit **Leading ExpertsTV.com** for more information.

Printing/Mailing Services

West Press

Kristy Scharf, phone **(888) 637-0337** or visit **WestPress.com.**

McClung Companies

Tom Trevillian, phone **(540) 949-8139** or visit **McClungCo.com.**

City Print (Division of City Blue Print)

Steven Harshbarger, phone **(316) 267-5555** or visit **CityBlue.com.**

Handy Mailing Services

Vergil Esau, phone **(316) 944-6258** or visit **HandyMailing.com.**

Advantage Media Group

Adam Witty, phone **(843) 414-5600** or visit **AdvantageFamily.com.**

Datum Direct

Dave Brady, phone **(312) 492-8822.**

Pete the Printer

Pete Lillo, visit **PeteThePrinter.com.**

Packaging/Promotional Products

American Retail Supply

For advertising aids, product packaging or items to insert into mailings to grab your prospects' attention, call American Retail Supply at **(800) 426-5708** or visit **MakeYouHappy.com** for ideas.

Copywriters

Michele PW

Phone **(877) 754-3384**; fax **(877) 754-3384.**

Mike Marasco

Phone **(928) 266-6745**; fax **(866) 486-7445.**

Daniel Levis

Phone **(705) 424-3232**; fax **(705) 424-9968.**

Information Resources

The Ultimate Shortcut ...

... for success and profitability in information marketing.

Every month, hundreds of startups turn to the Information Marketing Association to get their businesses started quickly. With its two monthly newsletters, *Best Practices in Information Marketing* monthly call and a monthly *Get Started Quick* coaching call for those just starting out, there is no better tool to make your business profitable. And for a limited time, it's *free.*

Readers of this book can join the Information Marketing Association for *free* by visiting **GetIMAFree.com** today. You may cancel your membership at any time. There is no obligation. Over the next two months, you will have the opportunity to enjoy all the membership benefits that our members already enjoy.

Info-Marketers' A-Z Blueprint Seminar ...

... for anyone who's in or wants to be in the *highly profitable* business of providing information.

Here's a partial list of topics discussed by Bill Glazer at the Information Marketing Business Development Blueprint Seminar

1. Seven decisions the new info-marketer needs to make:
   - How to evaluate a niche or subculture market
   - How to thoroughly profile the prospective customer
   - How to leverage the affinity you have with a niche
   - How to create a relationship with a niche with which you have no affinity
   - How to get testimonials when you just start out in a niche
   - How to get great testimonials from customers/members
   - How to use your lead generation strategies to give you a whole lot more information about your market than merely new leads
2. A close look at a beginning, simple marketing funnel
3. An inside look at the six-year evolution of Bill's Marketing Funnel
4. An inside look at Bill's 2004 Marketing Funnel
5. How to create joint ventures that produce good leads at bargain cost

13. How to work effectively with trade journals and associations
14. How to systemize and automate the entire marketing funnel
15. How to grow rapidly with minimum staff
16. How to find the right staff for an info-marketing business (Number-one headache, I hear!)
17. When to give up the front end and concentrate on the back end
18. The easiest ways to create back-end products
19. Different coaching program models to consider
20. Outside-the-box lead generation strategies (like "The Industry Survey")
21. Successful uses of audiotapes and CDs as sales tools
22. How to sell via trade shows, seminars and speaking opportunities
23. How to (legally) use broadcast fax
24. How to mine unconverted leads 12 to 36 months after acquisition
25. How to build the most saleable info-products/kits
26. How to minimize refunds
27. How to maximize referrals
28. The Complete Business Blueprint: used for Bill's BGS Marketing business
29. How to maximize profits and customer value with "forced continuity"
30. How to front-end a newsletter
31. How an "offline guy" uses the internet painlessly and profitably
32. An inside look at the financial truths of info-businesses: actual revenues, costs, profits, etc. (real case histories)
33. How to identify missed opportunities in your info-business plan
34. Seven most frequently made mistakes to avoid
35. How to expand from one niche to multiple niches—how I'm doing it now

36. How to negotiate with media to make sure you get the best deal—even after they already said you've got the best price
37. How to analyze new vendors to avoid a business nightmare
38. Copywriting formulas and shortcuts—Bill will give you his own copywriting questionnaire that he personally uses before he writes any copy for a client or himself. Frank discussion on outsourcing vs. doing it in-house (the pros and cons)
39. When do you give up on a niche?

While Bill Glazer's A–Z course is normally a $697 investment, as a reader of this book, you can get the online version of this program *free*. Visit **QuickInfoMarketing.com** for details.

Index

Index

Index

Index

Index